KNITTING IN THE
NORDIC TRADITION

KNITTING IN THE NORDIC TRADITION

VIBEKE LIND

English translation by
Annette Allen Jensen

Lark Books
Asheville, North Carolina

Library of Congress Cataloging-in-Publication Data

[Stik med nordisk tradition. English]
    Knitting in the Nordic tradition / Vibeke Lind : English translation
by Annette Allen Jensen.
        p.   cm.
    Translation of: Strik med nordisk tradition.
    Includes index.
    ISBN 1-887374-31-0 (pbk.)
    1. Knitting--Scandinavia.   I. Title.
TT819.S26L5613   1997
746.43'20432'0948--dc21

96-40236
CIP

10 9 8 7 6 5 4 3 2 1

Published by Lark Books,
50 College St., Asheville, NC 28801

Originally published as Vibeke Lind, *Strik med Nordisk Tradition,*
Host & Søns Forlag, 1981

English translation © 1997, Lark Books

Distributed in the U.S by Sterling Publishing Co., Inc.
    387 Park Ave. South, New York, NY 10016; 1-800-367-9692

Distributed in Canada by Sterling Publishing,
    c/o Canadian Manda Group, One Atlantic Ave.,
    Suite 105, Toronto, Ontario, Canada M6K 3E7

Distributed in Great Britain and Europe by Cassell PLC,
    Wellington House, 125 Strand, London, England WC2R 0BB

Distributed in Australia by Capricorn Link (Australia) Pty Ltd.,
    P.O. Box 6651, Baulkham Hills Business Centre, NSW, Australia 2153

Printed in Hong Kong

ISBN 1-887374-31-0

Contents

Wool for knitting

Possibilities with knitting

Sweaters and shirts

Shawls and scarves

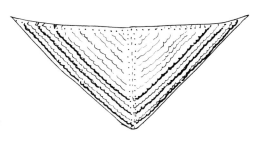

Caps

Mittens

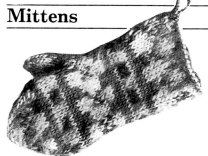

Stockings

Treatment of woollen clothes

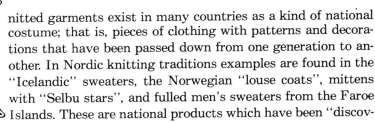

nitted garments exist in many countries as a kind of national costume; that is, pieces of clothing with patterns and decorations that have been passed down from one generation to another. In Nordic knitting traditions examples are found in the "Icelandic" sweaters, the Norwegian "louse coats", mittens with "Selbu stars", and fulled men's sweaters from the Faroe Islands. These are national products which have been "discovered" and turned into tourist items. As time passes, these articles tend to become more expensive and less well made. The emphasis is laid on the decorative effect and not, as originally, on the function of the article.

The general decline of handicrafts is not only the result of technological development, it is also the last stage in a complicated historical and social course. For economic reasons, it is difficult to cultivate handicrafts as anything but hobbies. Nevertheless, interest in learning from the old handicrafts continues to grow stronger.

For this reason I have tried to present a pictorial overview of different basic models of sweaters, jackets, caps, mittens, stockings, and shawls for children and adults.

The models shown and described are simple in cut and decoration. They are characteristic of Nordic knitting principles and pattern forms, based on practical and aesthetic values.

The purpose of the book is not to give the reader the patterns themselves, but rather to suggest how one can use the models, changing them according to individual needs and the dictates of fashion. They should be an inspiration to independent judgement of old ideas.

An artist does not always use patterns just for the sake of decoration. Decoration can be used to emphasize a shape or to mark progress. The fixed points in the composition of a pattern can be used as springboards for further development of the pattern. Fixed points can also serve to relieve the mind. Playing with form and material in this way, it is possible to renew oneself and to sharpen one's intellect.

Vibeke Lind

Wool for knitting

Having the right yarn for the work is a must, and under the Nordic skies it has been natural from early times to use the wool of sheep. For one thing, wool has been readily available, and for another, wool has many qualities that are valuable in the climate.

Woolen clothes give a comfortable warmth in cold weather but can also seem cool on a warm summer day. The millions of tiny air pockets formed by the frizzy fibers that make up the woollen thread provide excellent insulation.

A knitted textile is very elastic, and the wool fibers themselves are elastic, too. A wool fiber can be stretched to more than 50% of its original length and contract to its normal length again. This elasticity makes a woollen garment relatively wrinkle proof, and if it does wrinkle, the creases will usually hang out.

Sheep are out in all kinds of weather. If it rains, the water rolls off their coats. Some of the natural oil in the untreated wool is preserved in the knitting yarn and makes it water repellent. Still, wool can absorb up to 40% of its weight in water without feeling damp. It also absorbs body moisture easily.

From wool to yarn

The sheep are sheared once or twice a year, depending on the breed. There is a difference between annual and semi-annual wool.

This old photograph of sheep shearers from the Faroe Islands shows how wool was used in many ways. The men are dressed in woolen garments from top to toe.

Before the wool can be treated, it must be cleaned. Oil, sweat, plant scraps, and other particles can be removed by washing the wool care-fully in soft water. Long ago the sheep themselves were washed before being sheared because it was easier to dry the wool while still on the animal.

Different breeds of sheep produce different types of wool. Some breeds have thin, frizzy wool and others have straight, coarse wool.

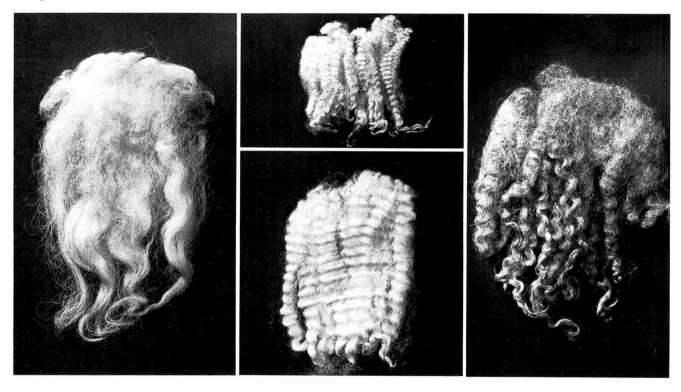

The wool of a sheep's coat is not uniform. It varies according to where it grows on the sheep's body. Usually the best wool comes from the shoulders and sides. Much experience is required to learn to sort and evaluate the wool.

The Gotland outdoor sheep shown here is a breed that is sheared annually. The coat comes off in one piece because the fat content and the kinkiness cause it to hang together.

10

Spinning principles

The wool can be spun according to two different principles: worsted spinning and card yarn spinning.

Worsted yarn is spun from particularly long fibers that are stretched and combed; any short fibers are combed out. The long fibers are arranged parallel to one another so that the thread becomes smooth and firm when spun. Worsted yarn is considered the most durable.

For card yarn, short, kinky fibers are used. Weak and strong fibers are mixed together in the process of carding the wool. Card wool is not stretched; the fibers are not parallel to one another. The result is an airy, fuzzy yarn which is warm but not especially strong.

When worsted is knit the threads can be seen easily and the patterns stand out clearly.

The patterns are more diffuse and blurry when knit with the "fuzzy" card yarn. If the knitwear is brushed up or fulled it will become so thick and close that the stitches will be completely concealed.

If you wish to use a stronger and more even yarn, you can spin two or more threads together. The small irregularities that are sometimes found in spun yarn disappear if the yarn is twisted.

The long fibers are combed parallel.

The card wool is mixed between the fine steel teeth of the carding boards.

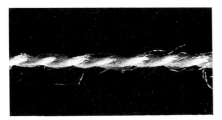

Double worsted.

Double card yarn.

A tapestry entitled "Work in the Smoke Room", sewn by Beata and Petra Petersen from Sandi, the Faroe Islands. It shows yarnmaking as it was done in the Faroe community only 30 or 40 years ago.

The significance of yarn

How the yarn is spun and twisted, whether it is thick or thin, soft or hard, determines the appearance of knitwear. The success of a piece is dependent upon how well the yarn and the method of knitting are combined.

There will always be unexplored combinations of knitting patterns and yarn qualities. The endless variations of knitting forms in connection with the structure of the yarn produce many different qualities, which can be typed from hard wearing to light and airy.

Shown here are some examples of typical yarn qualities and patterns that are often found in the Nordic knitting tradition.

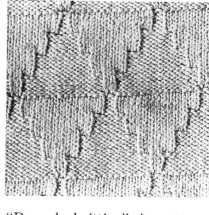

"Damask knitting" is patterns knit with the help of purl stitches, which stand out in relief against a stockinette stitch background. The technique is used to copy woven damask motifs. The patterns are seen most clearly when they are knit tightly with smooth yarn.

Diagonal knitting. Knit with an even number of stitches. 1st row: purl. 2nd row: the second stitch is knit before the first stitch, the fourth before the third, etc. to the end of the row. 3rd row: purl. 4th row: k 1, knit third stitch before second, the fifth before the fourth, etc. End the row with a knit stitch. Repeat these four rows.

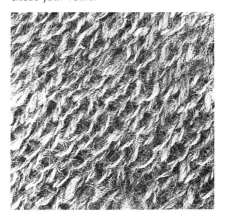

A plain pattern for everyday use taken from an old Danish men's sweater (alternate: one row knit, one row k 1, p 1). The character of this pattern changes completely when many different yarns are used together.

Multicolored knitting in an old Norwegian border design, natural black on a white background. Using fine yarn and thin needles, you can obtain a very clear design.

Unspun yarn that is brushed up after it has been knit creates an extra insulating layer in the knit work. Characteristic for Iceland is knitting with wool in its natural colors – white, light gray, and brownish black.

Pattern play in black and white. The machine-made yarn has purposely been given the unevenness characteristic of hand-spun yarn.

Diagonal knitting with hand-spun dog's hair. Interest in hand-spun yarn has grown immensely and many people experiment with spinning non-traditional materials. Still, it was not uncommon earlier to mix the hair of other animals with wool to make a stronger yarn.

Plain lace pattern knit with thin, single-thread Icelandic wool.

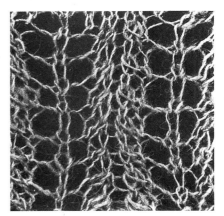

A lace pattern. Divisible by seven. 1st row: k 2 together, k 1. Wrap the yarn around the needle, k 1, yarn around needle, k 1, k 2 together by slipping one stitch off the needle and over the other, which has been knit. Repeat to the end of the row. 2nd row: purl. Repeat these two rows.

13

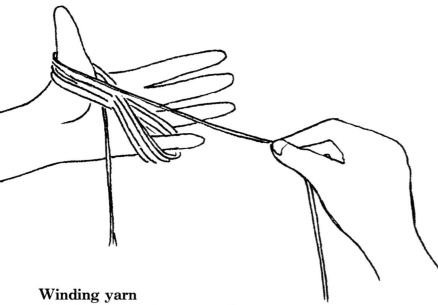

*"Front yarn"–
unspun yarn that
comes in sheets –
should be twisted
as it is wound.*

Winding yarn

Yarn bought in skeins must be wound into balls and this is best done so that the yarn comes out from the center of the ball while knitting.

First wind the yarn a few times around your second finger and the thumb of your left hand. Then fold the two loops together and wind the yarn around them while holding onto the short end. Be careful not to wind the yarn so tight that it stretches, for that may make the knitting uneven and too firm. Hold the ball by inserting your thumb in the center, continuing to hold the loose end. Turn the ball regularly so that it grows evenly, and every now and then, wrap the yarn a few times around your thumb at the base of the ball.

Finally, wind the yarn a few times around the middle and fasten the loose end here. This will prevent the ball from rolling away from you while knitting.

A ball wound in this way is also practical when you knit with two strands of yarn. You can use the yarn from the center and from the outside at the same time.

A "gilli-hook" was used to fasten the yarn at the left shoulder so that one could knit as one wandered.

14

You can knit back and forth with a circular needle or with several needles in a row if you have a large numbers of stitches.

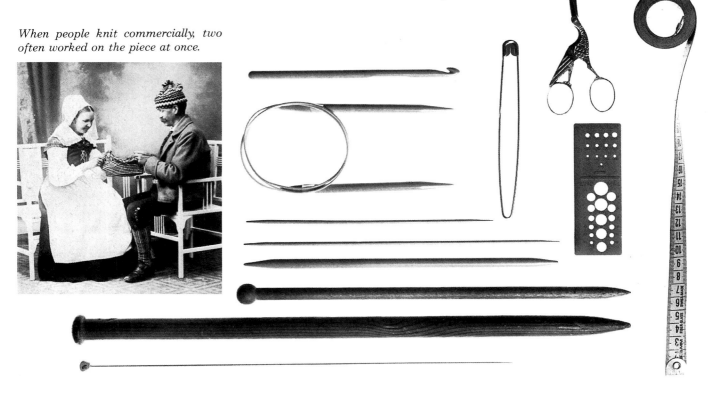

Tools

All that is needed to knit is yarn and needles. You should select the knitting needles according to the kind of knitting you plan to do; there are many possibilities. With two needles you can knit back and forth. To knit in rounds, four or five needles tapered at both ends are required, or a circular needle. The circular needle is of recent origin. Earlier as many as ten needles were used to make a circular-knit sweater.

It is a good idea to have a large assortment of needles on hand in various materials and sizes. For certain kinds of knitting, the needles should not be too slippery and wooden needles would be preferable.

In some patterns it is very important to be able to change from one needle size to another. Increasing and decreasing can be avoided in some cases by using thicker or thinner needles. It is common to use thinner needles for the thumbs of mittens and the heels of socks to make the knitting firmer and improve the wearing quality.

When you try to gather a set of stocking needles, it can be difficult to see whether they are all the same size. You can test them by making a hole in a piece of paper with each needle and measuring the holes to see if the diameters are the same. Additionally, you can control whether or not the needles and the yarn harmonize by passing the yarn end through the hole made by the needle. You can purchase several kinds of tools for measuring needles that will give the sizes in millimeters.

Finally, objects like a pair of scissors, a measuring tape, stitch holders, crochet hooks and the like are practical to have on hand.

When people knit commercially, two often worked on the piece at once.

About patterns

How many stitches and what size needle one should use for a certain pattern depends on the individual. Most people have probably discovered that a garment knit with a given number of stitches either ends up being much larger or smaller than expected.

Some people knit loosely and others tightly, and only the most experienced are able to maintain an even tension throughout the whole work. Both physical and psychological conditions can be influential; weather and fatigue can hamper the free movement of your fingers. The patterns shown in this book are therefore simple in shape, and the size of the needles and the type of yarn are given. Possible difficulties are described and the technical details that are emphasized are discussed thoroughly. For the inexperienced it is helpful to be able to concentrate on patterns and colors and learning to trust one's own judgement rather than to become involved with complicated fittings.

The expert should, from his or her experience and understanding, be able to use the models shown for inspiration and go on to change, improve, and invent new models from the basic ones.

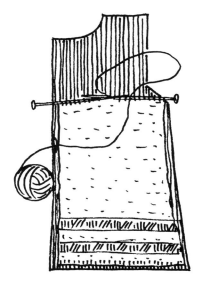

It is possible to knit from a sewing pattern. Do not allow for seams; on the contrary, knit short of the seamline because of the knit work's elasticity. Draw the pattern in full size and with both front or back pieces together, not in halves as you do in sewing.

Remember!

It is important to make calculations, to knit gauge swatches and compare the results. Before you start a piece of knitting, you should know how many stitches and rows there are in one centimeter. Naturally you have to knit a larger sample in order to make an exact measurement. The small diagrams shown with the models are guides to how many stitches across and how many rows it takes to make ten square centimeters.

Before you measure a gauge swatch let it rest a few hours so that the yarn can retract to its original structure.

Symbols

If you describe a knitting pattern only in words, misunderstandings can easily arise. That is why stitch symbols and diagrams are used.

At the same time it is convenient to have simple symbols for the most common knitting stitches when you want to record your own experiments.

Beside each pattern, there is a key to the symbols used.

Symbols for knitting in rounds.

Key to symbols
V = 1 knit stitch
∩ = 1 purl stitch

```
∩ ∩ ∩ ∩  4.
∩ V V V  3.
∩ V V V  2.
∩ V V V  1.
```

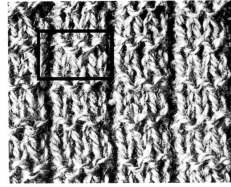

1st three rows: k 3, p 1
4th row: p
The code follows the knitting direction and is read from right to left.

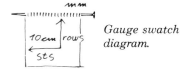

Gauge swatch diagram.

Repeats

When you want to illustrate a pattern, it is most clear when repeated once or twice, but as you follow the directions you need only the number of stitches and rows that comprise one repeat.

Some patterns are best illustrated like cross-stitch patterns, where one square equals one stitch. This system can be used for either multicolored knitting or damask knitting where you alternate knit and purl stitches.

For other knitting patterns symbols are used to indicate different stitches.

Symbols for knitting back and forth.

4. ∨ ∨ ∨ ∨
∩ ∨ ∨ ∨ 3.
2. ∨ ∩ ∩ ∩
∩ ∨ ∨ ∨ 1.

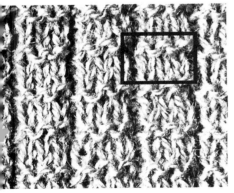

1st row: k 3, p 1
2nd row: k 1, p 3
3rd row like 1st row.
4th row: k

When a pattern is repeated, either across or vertically, the pattern is called "a repeat".

A simple pattern, like a square, that is two stitches wide and two rows long, repeats horizontally when you have knit four stitches and it repeats vertically when you have knit four rows.

A slightly more complicated repeat is the star figure. It has a repeat of eighteen stitches and sixteen rows.

Possibilities with knitting

Knit work has a distinctive elastic quality that allows a garment to take the shape of the body. What's more, knitting technique makes it possible to shape a work without cutting. In order to control the design it is necessary to know the basic elements of knitting.

Knitting and purling

It is questionable whether there are one or two basic stitches in knitting, for a knit stitch automatically forms a purl stitch on the wrong side of the work. Not until one purposely alternates knit stitches and purl stitches can one exploit their possibilities creatively. These two stitches are the basis of all more or less complicated and ingenious knitting techniques.

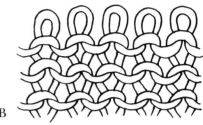

Stockinette stitch, right side.

Stockinette stitch, wrong side.

To knit stockinette stitch use either circular needles and knit stitch in rounds, or use two needles and alternate one row knit, one row purl. Stockinette gives a distinct, smooth, vertically striped effect on the right side and a horizontal pattern on the wrong side.

Vertical effects
Looking closely at the right side of a stockinette stitch work, you will observe a slightly grooved vertical stripe. The knitting is elastic in the width. This effect is heightened by ribbing. The wider the ribbing, the deeper the grooves.

Stockinette stitch. See A above.

Narrow ribbing. Knit one, purl one across all rows. The knitting contracts slightly.

Wide ribbing. Knit five, purl five. The knit stitches stand out and emphasize the vertical effect. The knitting contracts markedly.

If you wish to give the knitting more stability, you must reduce the elasticity of the ribbing. The simplest way is to stagger the ribbing at regular intervals.

Reducing the elasticity of ribbing.

Horizontal and vertical effects emphasized and the knitting stabilized.

Horizontal effects

The wrong side of a stockinette stitch work has a distinct horizontal pattern, contrary to the vertically striped appearance of the right side.

If you wish to emphasize the horizontal effect, use the so-called garter stitch that is done by knitting only knit stitches, back and forth; or knit in rounds alternating one row of knitting and one row of purling. The right and wrong sides will be identical.

Stockinette stitch. See B, upper left.

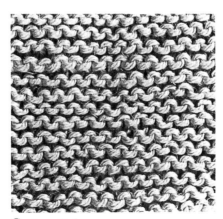

Garter stitch.

You achieve a horizontal effect when you alternate the right and wrong sides of a piece knit in stockinette. Here the change is made every tenth row. The "wrong side" stitches dominate the right.

Decorative patterns with knit and purl stitches

Many knitting patterns have their origin in an attempt to copy other textile techniques, most frequently weaving. In Denmark purl stitches have commonly been used on a stockinette background to form patterns. Many of the patterns were taken from damask cloths in which the most is made of the difference between rough and smooth surfaces, the characteristics of right and wrong sides of the fabric.

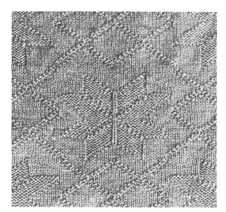

A typical pattern from the sleeve of an old nightshirt from Roesnaes, Denmark. The star pattern was one of the

most common in Skaane and Denmark. The pattern is used in the sweater on page 42.

Free garter stitch knitting

By working with just knit stitches in many variations, you can achieve unexpected results that you eventually will be able to obtain deliberately. If you use double-pointed needles, you can start each row with a new yarn as you wish. By shifting between thick and thin needles, irregularly spun yarn and fine yarn, you can develop other variations. You can increase and decrease as you please as long as you keep the same total number of stitches. Maintain the balance at all times. The larger the piece of knitting, the greater the distance can be between repeats.

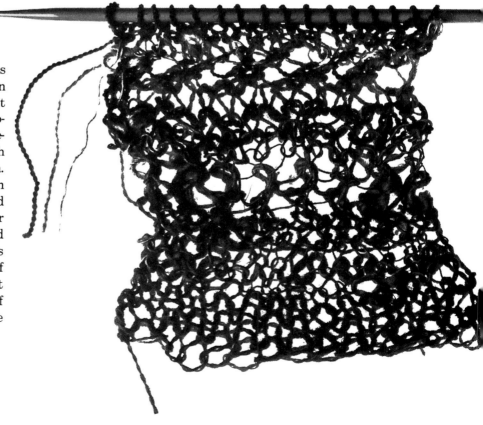

20

Shaping by increasing and decreasing

You can shape a garment as you knit it. You can make it larger by increasing the number of stitches or smaller by decreasing.

Additionally you can use increasing and decreasing in a decorative manner – to make a zigzag pattern or a slanting pattern – as long as you remember to add the number you subtract, or vice versa, if you want to maintain the same total number of stitches.

Horizontal zigzagging

You can make a zigzag border like the one seen below by increasing and decreasing. Basically this pattern is the same as that seen at the lower right on page 19; however, you increase and decrease during the first five rows of the repeat.

A zigzag pattern used as decoration on the cuff of a glove.

Knit bias tape

This sample is knit with six stitches. 1st row: slip the 1st stitch onto the right needle, pick up the strand that joins the 1st and 2nd stitches with the left needle and knit it like a turned knit stitch, then k 3, slip 1 stitch, k 1, pass the slipped stitch over the knit stitch. 2nd row: purl. Repeat these two rows.

Vertical zigzagging

A vertical zigzag design is shown in this openwork pattern. You can shift from a right to a left slant

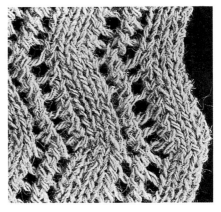

and vice versa by following these two repeats: wrap the yarn around the needle, k 2 stitches together twice, wrap the yarn around the needle. 2nd row: purl. In this sample the slant is changed every seventh row.

2. ∩∩∩∩∩∩∩∩ *Slant to*
V O ◢ O ◢ V V V 1. *right.*

2. ∩∩∩∩∩∩∩∩ *Slant to*
◣ O ◣ O V V V V 1. *the left.*

Key to symbols

O = wrap yarn around needle
V = 1 knit stitch
∩ = 1 purl stitch
◢ = 2 stitches together
◣ = 2 stitches together through back of loop
Ѷ = 1 stitch through front of loop 1 stitch through back of loop

Openwork knitting

To obtain a loose, openwork effect you can make eyelets in the knitting by increasing and decreasing an equal number of stitches. In the simplest form, the pattern calls for eyelets that are close together, all knit on the same row so as to maintain the same total number of stitches.

The more complicated patterns may call for increasing a number of times in one row and decreasing correspondingly several rows later.

In some patterns you increase and decrease only on the right side of the work while you simply knit or purl on the wrong side. In others, you increase and decrease on both sides.

The most common way to increase is to wrap the yarn around the needle because this makes the desired eyelet in the knitting, but there are several ways to decrease, each of which has its own decorative effect.

By using these different techniques in various combinations, you can knit lace.

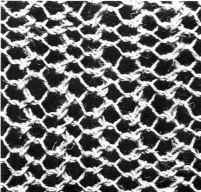

Pattern effects on both the right and wrong sides

By repeating two movements continuously – wrap the yarn around the needle, knit two together – on both right and wrong sides, you achieve a net-like open effect.

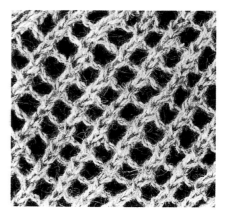

Pattern effects on only one side

If you use the same two stitch combinations – wrap the yarn around the needle, knit two together – but only on the right side of the knitting, the pattern will be at a slant to the right or the left, depending upon whether the wrapping is done before or after the decreasing.

To reduce the slant, alternate between one row of wrapping first and one row of decreasing first.

Eyelet

It is clear from the two previous examples that "wrap the yarn around the needle, knit two together" makes holes in the knitting. If you want to have a vertical row of distinct eyelet, you should knit three rows of stockinette stitch between each row of eyelet.

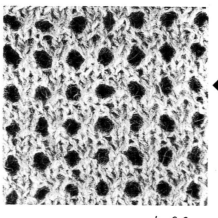

Large eyelet

An eyelet can be made larger by knitting two, three, or even more stitches in the 'same wrapping on the return row, just as you can make the wrapping more open by turning the yarn around the needle twice.

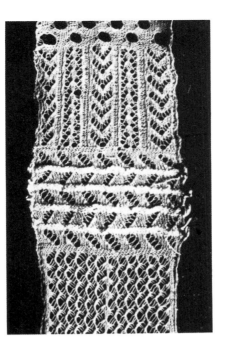

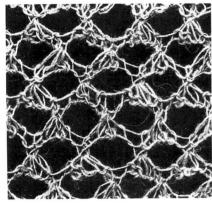

The number of stitches in this pattern is divisible by four. The work should be supported at the edges with – for example – at least two extra stitches at each edge.

1st row: wrap around, p 4 stitches together. 2nd row: k 1, through the wrapping k 1, p 1, k 1. 3rd row: with a needle twice as big as the others, knit.

The knitting sample seen in this photograph is one of 83 old patterns kept at the Nordenfjeldske Museum of Decorative Arts in Trondheim, Norway. The samples, which are knit successively in one long row 4 meters long and 6 centimeters wide, are made with fine, white, very tightly twisted cotton yarn. They demonstrate how patterns were preserved long ago and passed on.

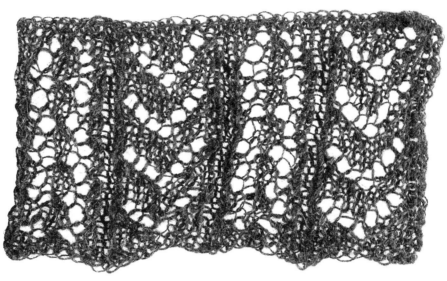

Key to symbols

O = wrap yarn around needle
V = 1 knit stitch
∩ = 1 purl stitch
◢ = 2 stitches together
◣ = 2 stitches together through back of loop
▲ = 3 stitches together

The even return rows are purled where no other instruction is given.

```
V V O ◢ O V V   ∩ ∩  5.
◢ O V V V O ◣   ∩ ∩  3.
◢ O V V V O ◣   ∩ ∩  1.
```

```
◣ O V V V V V O ◢ ∩ ∩  7.
V ◣ O V V V O ◢ V ∩ ∩  5.
V V ◣ O V O ◢ V V ∩ ∩  3.
V V V ◣ O V V V V V ∩ ∩  1.
```

In the above old sample two very simple patterns are combined to form vertical stripes joined by two purl stitches. For clarity's sake the two patterns are shown separately because the first repeats every fifth row and the second repeats every seventh row. On page 88 the V-shaped pattern is used in a cap.

Multicolored knitting

Multicolored knitting is characteristic of Scandinavian work. The design is often geometric with either vertical or horizontal stripes or with small, simple motifs that are repeated at short intervals.

Some motifs are several hundred years old. Originally the wool was used in its natural colors – white to light brown to black – but now and then red, indigo blue, and different plant dyes were used.

A choice example of multicolored knitting. In a number of the patterns three strands are used in the same row. The mittens are from Finnmark, Norway.

The technique

Most frequently the knitting is done with two different colors at once, and the color that is not used is carried along the wrong side of the knitting. The work acquires the character of woven cloth and loses some of its elasticity, but it has another important quality, for the material is double thickness and thus insulates better.

In Scandinavia nowadays one carries the knitting yarn over the left index finger. Earlier it was common to knit with the yarn over the right index finger.

On the Faroe Islands, where they still keep up many of the old traditions, they combine the two methods in multicolored knitting: they hold one yarn with the right index finger and the other with the left.

Multicolored knitting is easiest to work in rounds so that you can see the pattern at all times and avoid rows of purling.

Generally the patterns are designed so that the space between color changes is only a few stitches and you merely have to take care that the yarn is carried lightly and untangled on the wrong side between changes. If there are many stitches between each change of color, you should twist the two strands on the wrong side. See also page 107.

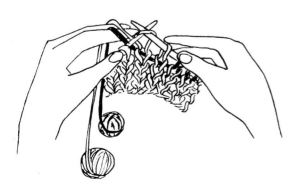

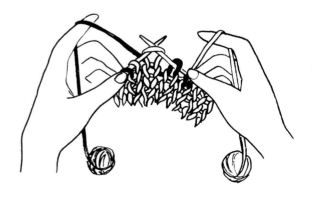

Fascinating play with colors. ▶

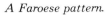
A Faroese pattern.

An example of a pattern with three colors. Notice that only two colors are used in a single row.

There are times when you need to knit back and forth. Then it is necessary to bring both strands to the ends of the rows and fasten them so that the yarn always runs horizontally. You can manage this by knitting the last stitch in each row with both colors – or *all* the colors that have been used in the row in question. In the following row, slip the first stitch onto the right needle and thereafter continue the pattern.

In Scandinavian knitting you rarely see a pattern in which more than seven stitches occur between color changes. It is advisable to limit the distance to five stitches so that fingers and buttons do not get caught in the threads.

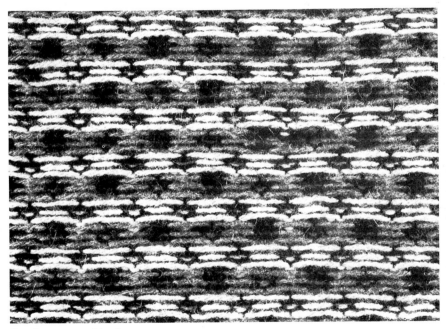

On the wrong side the yarn runs evenly and regularly.

◀ *A great variety of patterns can be made by experimenting with colors.*

Scandinavian patterns

A common feature of Scandinavian knitting patterns is the use of small geometric figures like dots, triangles, squares, rhombuses, and crosses. In addition to these basic elements, the star and rose patterns are employed, as is often the case in textile arts.

Some patterns carry the names of certain districts or valleys like the Norwegian "Selbu-star" that is known far and wide. In other cases the natural environment has inspired and lent names to the patterns, "Sea-wave" and "Sheep's Path" from the Faroe Islands, for example.

Formerly, old magic could be hidden in a pattern. The heathen sunwheel gave rise to some patterns, and Christian symbols like the cross and stars often served as the basis for other popular patterns.

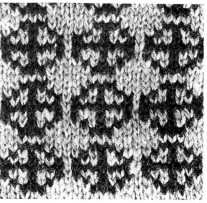

Spinning Wheel.

Could this pattern, which is called "Spinning Wheel" on the Faroes, be an old sun symbol?

Concepts like stars, snow flakes, night and day, are popular as pattern names. These patterns are both called "Night and Day". One is from Gotland and the other from the Faroe Islands.

Sun symbol from Gotland.

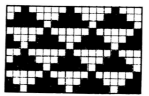

Gotland.

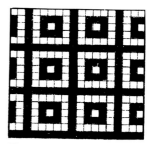

The Faroe Islands.

In some places the pattern above is called "Cat's Paw", but it could just as well have derived from the old sun symbol pattern from Gotland.

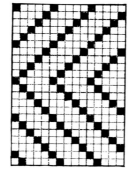

Sheep's Path.

Patterns like "Sea-wave" and "Sheep's Path" are characteristic of Faroese knitting. See also page 52.

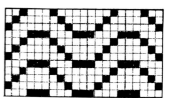

Sea-wave.

26

The *"Strawberry Flower"* pattern comes from Gotland.

Fisherman from the Faroe Islands.

Snowflake.

Little Star.

Stars and nets

The simplest pattern is a very popular background motif; it consists of a single stitch that looks like a dot in a different color and the dots are staggered at regular intervals with more or less space between them. The closer the dots are placed, the more stable and compact the knit work will be.

A development of this pattern is a small star, also placed at close or distant intervals. The diagonal or net-like effect can be emphasized, or the star figure can be made even larger; but the larger the figure, the more detailed the design must be so that the distance between the yarn changes is not too great.

In addition to its aesthetic value, the diagonal design has a practical function: it stabilizes the knitting because the two strands of yarn are alternated regularly in each row.

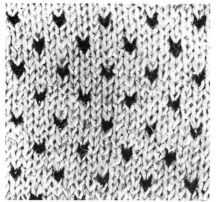

Dots or "lice" can be of different colors in every other row or can be knit with a thinner yarn for effect.

Small stars can be knit light on a dark background or the other way around, and with more or less space between them.

Stars with dots between them.

The dots can be gathered into a net.

28

Stars close together, or a net?

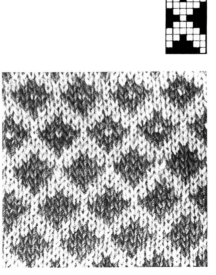

Big Star is an old motif from the Faroes.

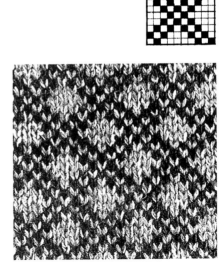

Big star with double net.

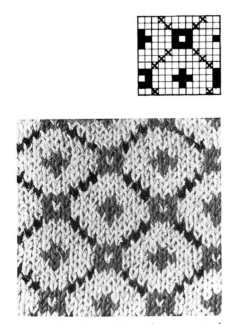

The net is of one color and is connected by squares of another. Pattern from the Faroes.

The star is among the oldest motifs in knitting, also in weaving and embroidery.

Wheel pattern – sunwheel. From an old mitten from Gotland, near the east coast of Sweden

29

Casting on and off

You can start and end a piece of knitting in many more ways than you would think. Sometimes the edges must be elastic, as at the top of a sock, or firm so that they can stand wear; at other times the decorative effect is the decisive factor.

There are two main methods of casting on: the one-needle method and the two-needle method. Endless variations, each with its own distinct character, can be made with these.

To make loose stitches you should cast on over two needles at once.

Ordinary casting on with one needle

Take a suitable length of yarn – enough to make the number of stitches required – and make the first loop. Move the needle around the yarn in the direction of the arrows. Withdraw the thumb from the loop and tighten the yarn.

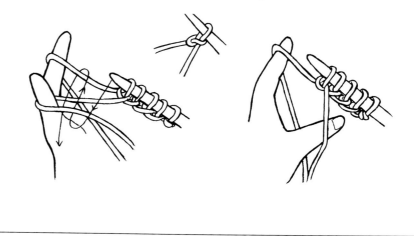

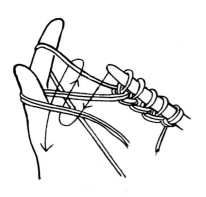

You can make the lower edge of the stitches thicker by doubling the thumb yarn or using two strands.

The ordinary one-needle method, seen from the right side. Additional effects are obtained by using double yarn for casting on and by knitting the second row.

The ordinary one-needle method, seen from the wrong side. The stitches are cast on with double yarn, the first row is purled, and the rest of the rows are knit in stockinette.

The one-needle method with triple yarn

The edge is very strong when cast on with a tripled "thumb yarn".

Loop the thumb yarn so that it consists of three strands. Insert the right needle in the loop, draw the three strands acoss your left thumb and the knitting yarn across your left index finger. Cast on as usual.

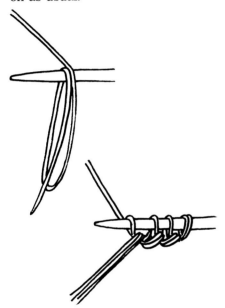

The one-needle method using two colors

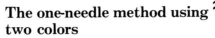

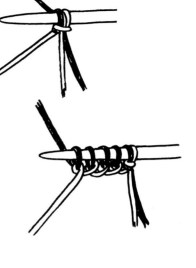

When you are going to knit with more than one color, you can cast on with two. The color of the yarn held over your thumb will be the color of the bottom edge.

You can vary the color of this edge, for example by alternating between a dark and a light colored yarn across your thumb. In this case the edge will be two-colored.

The double one-needle method with triple yarn

If you cast on two stitches before you tighten the thumb yarn the result will look like this. In other words, you cast on the second stitch using the back strand of the thumb yarn.

The two-needle method, or "school method"

Make a loop and place it on the left needle, knit a stitch (fig. 1 and 2), place it back on the left needle, turned (fig. 3). Continue knitting as shown (fig. 4 and 5), working through the last stitch, putting the new stitch back on the left needle.

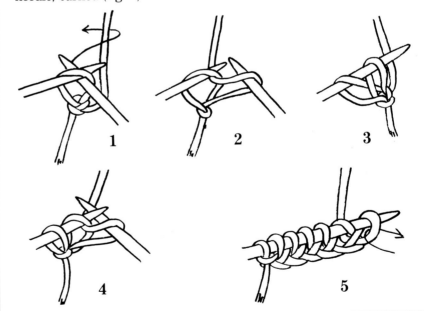

1   **2**   **3**

4   **5**

A variation of school casting on is made by inserting the needle between the last two stitches, wrapping the yarn around the needle and setting the stitch up on the left needle as before. In this case the edge will be thicker and stronger.

31

Lace casting on

Like school casting on, lace casting on is knit with two needles, but instead of knitting a certain number of stitches along the needle, you knit them vertically in rows of two. The result is like trim and you can make it as long as you like.

Lace casting on makes decorative borders suitable for delicate knitting.

Cast two knit stitches on the left needle as in school casting on. Hold the yarn forward and slip the first stitch onto the right needle (fig. 1). Knit the second stitch and pass the slipped stitch over it (fig. 2). In this way you have cast on a new stitch and combined two so that you still have two stitches on the needle. Turn over the knitting and work as before.

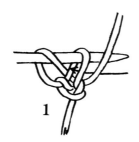

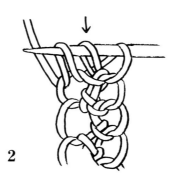

When the casting on is the desired length, cast off one by knitting the two stitches together, then pick up stitches through the loops of the strip.

This border is used for the hat on page 88.

If you cast on four stitches and continue the repeats, the result will look like the piece at the left.

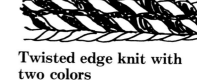

Twisted edge knit with two colors

A decorative but inflexible edge can be made by working the first two rows after casting on with twisted knitting.

This technique is not well known today, but here and there in the Nordic countries you will find it used for the borders on old stockings and mittens. There are even examples of knitwork made entirely with twisted knitting (see pages 105 and 109). Twisted knitting is done with two strands of yarn at a time, both of the same color or each a different color.

Seen above is an example of a

double border of twisted knitting.

In the example above the one needle casting on is done with two colors. After casting on, both strands are held in front of the work and knit alternately, first with one color and then the other.

For each stitch, bring the back

yarn forward from below and purl the stitch, turned (which is easiest). As you knit, the knitting yarn will become twisted and you will have to stop frequently to untangle it.

If you are knitting in rounds, you should twist the yarn in front of the work on the right side during the first two rounds. When you knit back and forth, you also twist the yarn on the right side of the work, which means that on the return row you should twist the yarn behind the work.

Twisted edge with three colors

The technique can be developed by using three colors. Here is a border in which the second row is knit in reverse: the yarn is taken from the center each time a stitch is knit.

The three strands are held in front of the work.

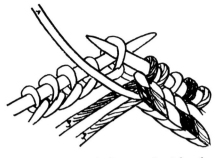

First purl one stitch, turned, with color 1. Then repeat with color 2, and finally with color 3. With each stitch the yarn is carried from below and up across the other two strands.

Crocheted casting on

A very simple way to cast on is to make a chain with a crochet hook of the same size as the knitting needles you plan to use. Then pick up one stitch in each loop of the chain.

Casting on new stitches to extend the knitting

To add many stitches to the knitting at one time, simply cast the new stitches on by holding the yarn over the thumb and index finger of your left hand. Then insert the right needle under the thumb yarn, lift the loop on to the needle and tighten the yarn as shown below.

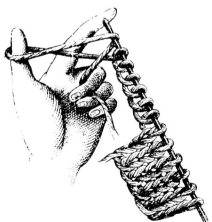

Casting on with waste yarn

At times invisible casting on is required, or you may want to cast off at both ends of the work so that they look alike. You can do this by knitting a few rows at the beginning of the work, which you will remove when the work is finished.

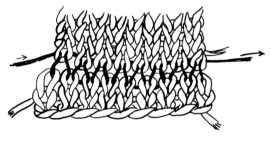

Cast on with waste yarn, just any remnant will do, and knit four or five rows. Then you change to another waste yarn – a strong, smooth one – and knit one row. Finally you begin the actual knitting with the chosen yarn.

When your knit work is finished, you pull the smooth yarn end and the first waste rows will fall off. Remaining will be the open stitches of the chosen yarn. These can be cast off or picked up, as you like.

Key to symbols
O = wrap yarn around needle
◣ = 2 stitches together through back of loop

33

About casting off

When you have finished a piece of knit work, the stitches should be fastened or cast off in one way or another. The casting off must not be too tight and in most cases it should be flexible. Therefore, you can cast off with a needle that is one or two millimeters thicker than the needles you used for knitting.

You can also loosen the casting off by knitting an extra stitch between two stitches at regular intervals on the casting off row.

The stitches you cast off should be knit like the pattern if nothing else is given: purl above purl and knit above knit.

Simple casting off

The easiest way to cast off a piece of knitting is to pull the yarn through the open stitches on the last row and tie the yarn to the last stitch. By using this method you can loosen or tighten the edges of the knitting by adjusting the tension of the yarn.

Chain casting off

The most common method leaves a row of stitches that look as if they have been sewn. This chain stitch edge is strong, it is quickly knit, and it is easy to undo if you want to make changes later on.

Knit the first two stitches and pass the first stitch over the second, so only the second stitch remains on the needle. Knit the third stitch and pass the second stitch over it. Continue to the end of the row until there is only stitch left. Break the yarn and draw the yarn end through the loop of the last stitch to close it.

Casting off by knitting stitches together

You can also knit two stitches together to make one, which you place back on the left needle. Knit two stitches together again and put the new stitch on the left

needle, as before. Repeat until all stitches have been cast off.

Sewing

Sewing can be used to join the open edges of a stockinette stitch work. A completely invisible seam can be made in this way, for instance on a shoulder. The number of stitches on the two pieces to be joined must be equal. See page 73 as well.

Edgings

Nowadays ribbed edges are especially common. As mentioned earlier, ribbing made by knitting 2 and purling 2, for example, is elastic, which is practical and useful particularly when you want a garment to fit tightly. Here are different edgings and decorative borders that show how many possibilities there are for variation if you dare move beyond conventional limits.

A simple and very popular pattern in Nordic knitting is one where a single stitch is emphasized by changing the color of yarn. In the Faroe Islands the motif is called "fleas" and in Norway "lice", which perhaps alludes to something about "the good old days". Below the motif is used in different ways, first as close-set "fleas" that gradually spread out vertically and horizontally, then as the Faroese Open Star. The number of stitches is increased by adding one stitch every other stitch.

Notice that even though the size of the needles used remains the same, the close-set fleas tighten the sleeve more than would a scattered pattern, and that the marked increase in the width of the sleeve follows the pattern.

Below is a sleeve edging where the number of stitches remains the same throughout the work even though the decorative pattern changes. By gradually changing the size of the needles, you can suitably narrow the sleeve.

The ribbing on the sleeve of a sweater can easily be turned into a muffette. Simply knit a horizontal hole 6 or 7 cm from the wrist.

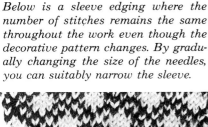

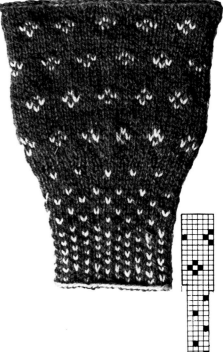

The lower edge will roll up if knit with ordinary stockinette stitch. Make the most of this and knit the first rows with smaller needles so that the cuff rolls up tighter. Here is a rolled cuff on a sweater with a decorative pattern created by alternating the wrong and right sides of stockinette stitch.

If you begin a piece of knitting by casting on with waste yarn, later you can knit, for example, a beautiful border at the bottom and on the cuffs. At the same time, you have a chance to lengthen the work, should you need to.

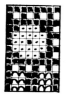

ⴖ = *purl*

After casting on with one needle and two colors (see page 31), knit the first round: p 1, then holding the yarn forward slip 1 stitch purl-wise onto the right needle, repeat to the end of the round. Second round: slip 1 stitch purl-wise onto the right needle holding the yarn forward, p 1. Repeat. The stitches will lie as light loops on the dark background. If the border is used as a pattern, the first pattern row should always have the same color as the previous one.

The edge made by twisted casting on with three colors, described in detail on page 33, is used here in connection with a simple border pattern.

Earlier, people were not hesitant to combine different patterns. To the right is a combination of two old motifs. Below is a pattern from a Danish man's stocking; above is a pattern used both in Norway and Estonia.

36

Sweaters and shirts

The basic model for a knit sweater is – in broad terms – a cylinder that is supplied with two smaller cylinders for sleeves. This basic model can be elaborated upon in different ways, depending on the knitting technique, on the type of yarn or the aesthetic criteria. The choice of materials and shapes is so vast that it seems as if there are too many options. When you prepare to knit a sweater, you should first decide which of the basic forms you will use – circular or plain knitting.

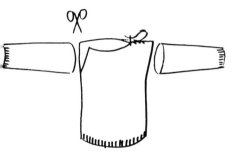

To achieve a better fit, you can knit the three cylinders – the body and two sleeves – together into one large piece and decrease until you reach the neck opening.

The use of more than one color in patterned knitting is mainly for the decorative effect, but apart from this, makes the fabric both warmer and more windproof. The technique is very suitable for knitting in rounds.

Knitting in rounds

By knitting in rounds you have the advantage of being able to see the right side of the work at all times, which is especially important when you work with counted-stitch patterns and multicolored knitting.

The armholes can simply be cut like slits in the knitted cylinder and the sleeves sewn on at the slits' edges. If you want the sweater open down the front, like a jacket, you also cut the knitting. The cut edges can be covered by knit front borders with buttons and buttonholes.

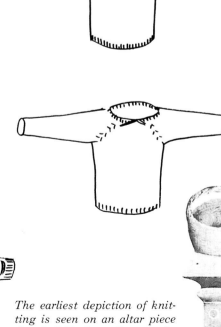

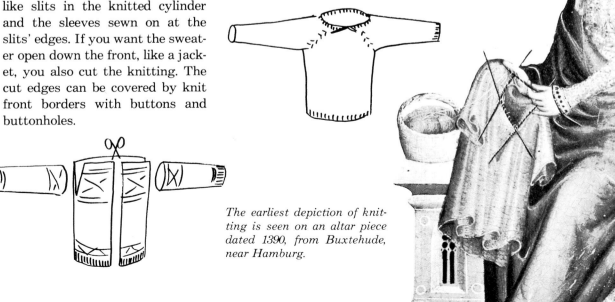

The earliest depiction of knitting is seen on an altar piece dated 1390, from Buxtehude, near Hamburg.

Flat knitting

The different pieces of a garment can be knit by following a pattern for sewing if you knit back and forth. Fine yarn and small-sized needles are best when using this technique because it is important that the seams do not bulge where the parts are joined.

Models that are knit according to this principle can easily be provided with pockets and collars.

When you knit back and forth, you can emphasize the vertical character (see also the passage on the possibilities of knitting, page 18) and make use of the elastic qualities by either knitting horizontally, as you normally do,

or by knitting vertically.

The simplest way to knit the sweater is to knit in one piece. Then you merely have to sew the side seams and the underside of the sleeves. However, if you wish to avoid large pieces you can try to make the seams form part of the sweater, keeping them as harmonious and elastic as possible.

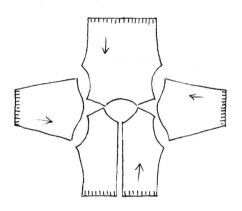 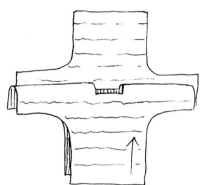 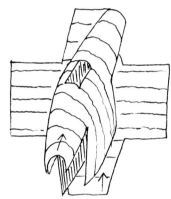

Measuring

Before you start knitting, you should take some measurements, make some calculations, and knit a gauge swatch with the needles and yarn you'll be using (see page 16).

Generally speaking, the proportions of the human body are identical, but it is easy to take individual differences into consideration as you calculate. As an example, shown here are the proportions of a normal outdoor sweater.

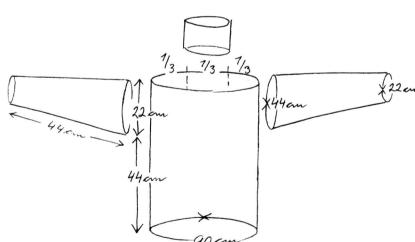

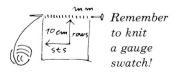

Remember to knit a gauge swatch!

All the measurements are taken in relation to the hip measurement. Generally, the sleeve width at the top is half of the hip measurement, and the sleeve width at the bottom is half of the sleeve width at the top.

As to the length of the sweater, you'll usually find that the depth of the armhole is one-third of the entire length, and that the under-sleeve length is the same as the length of the sweater from the bottom edge to the bottom edge of the armhole.

Your own model can be made by dividing and finely fitting this rough form.

Stockinette stitch plain sweater knit in rounds with cut armholes

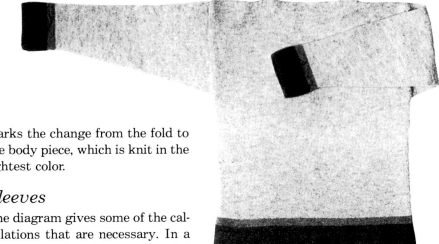

Following is a description of a plain sweater for which the measurements are worked out on the basis of general rules. This simple model can be made to fit almost anyone and importance is given to making as few seams and as few calculations as possible.

The whole sweater is knit in rounds with knit stitches only. The edges at the bottom and on the sleeves are folded inward, and the fold is knit with needles that are one size thinner, to hold the edges close to the body.

The neck opening is not shaped, which means that the sweater does not have a front or back side and the sleeves do not wear in the same place all the time.

To make the sweater durable, tightly twisted yarn is used. The finished sweater is washed and brushed thoroughly with a stiff brush, so that the wool fibers entangle lightly: this softens the sweater and at the same time gives it a greater insulating ability.

The colors of the sweater are the sheep's natural gray colors. The darkest gray is at the bottom and a narrow, middle gray stripe

marks the change from the fold to the body piece, which is knit in the lightest color.

Sleeves

The diagram gives some of the calculations that are necessary. In a gauge swatch, using needles, 2.5 mm, 29 stitches should make 10 cm. If this is the case, cast on 62 stitches for the bottom of the sleeves. After you have knit the sleeve border, increase on either side of the change from round to round, as shown on the detailed photograph on the following page. Here there are 4 stitches between the increases. Increase every 4th round, until the sleeve is the required length. This example is 45

cm long and has a total of 130 stitches at the top.

To allow for the seam, knit eight extra rounds before casting off – never too tightly. By knitting the sleeves first you will find your own knitting tension, and then you can correct your original knitting calculations.

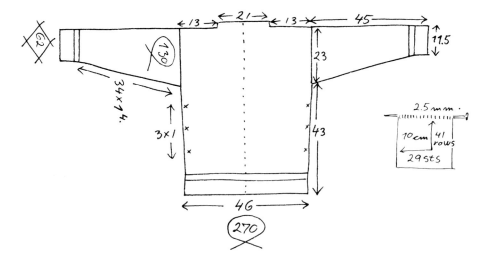

39

Increase strip

The photograph shows how the new stitch is made from the strand between two stitches, and therefore is completely independent of these and almost invisible. The increase is placed after the first two stitches of a round and before the last two stitches of the round so that the middle strip of four stitches forms the basis for decorative pattern details. See also page 42 and page 50.

The body

The body of the sweater is knit like the sleeves and is marked at both sides to show eventual increases and to show where the armholes will be later on.

If you are not sure how you want the bottom edge to look, or if you wish to decide the length later, you can cast on with waste yarn, which means yarn that can be removed so that you can knit in the other direction with the open stitches. (See page 33).

When the body is a suitable length, you can figure out the size of the neck opening by measuring your head.

Place the shoulder stitches on a stitch holder and knit about 3 cm with the remaining stitches. This piece will be folded into the neck opening; therefore, the first row should be purled so as to make a sharp edge.

When casting off, it is important not to do it too tightly. The best way is to sew the open stitches, one by one, onto the fabric.

Finishing

The shoulder stitches are knit together and cast off at the same time. This casting off gives a certain strength to the shoulder seam. After this the armhole slashes should be marked. Sew along either side of the marking on a sewing machine, and cut the knitting which now is held firmly by the machine stitching.

The sleeves are sewn onto the body. The eight extra rounds on the sleeves are sewed down on the wrong side to cover the seam.

The method of cutting the knit fabric is used especially in the Faroese and Norwegian sweaters, and it may seem brutal and against the nature of knitting, but it is much faster to work knit stitches the whole time, and the knitting easily

can become uneven if you knit back and forth from the armhole to the shoulder.

Knit casting off

Place the open stitches on two knitting needles. Turn the work inside out and hold the needles close together and parallel.

Knit two stitches together, one from each needle. Repeat. When two stitches have been knit, lift the first stitch over the second stitch as in ordinary casting off.

This casting off gives a firm and unelastic seam. If you wish to use a more flexible casting off, you can use the sewing method, (page 34).

Sweaters, clearly inspired by Nordic patterns.

Damask shirt – patterned knitting with knit and purl stitches

In old Danish knitting journals one often meets the term "tied night shirts", which really meant knitted, woollen sweaters. A night shirt was what one wore closest to the body, but not what we today know as underwear. The night shirts were the peasant women's copies of the elaborately knit blouses of the upper class.

In the seventeenth century it was fashionable for men in high social positions to wear knitted "undershirts" of silk, often richly embroidered with silver or gold threads.

The peasant woman's copy was made of firm, finely knit wool in the same characteristic star pattern seen over and over again in textile arts.

The night shirt was often worn under a small, tightly fitting waistcoat so that only the sleeves would show. The color was usually red, but sometimes bottle green, black or dark blue.

To the right is a raglan sweater with patterned borders in delicate, plant dyed shades. In the damask-knit smock to the left the pattern effect is heightened by the quality of the firmly twisted yarn.

◀

Distinguished silk blouse from Norway, probably from the 17th century. It is known that the British King Charles I was wearing a similar silk blouse when he was executed in 1649.

A girl wearing a Salling regional dress from the middle of the last century.

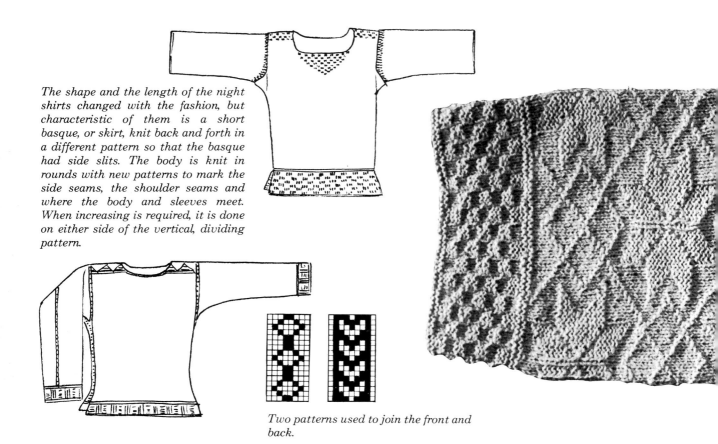

The shape and the length of the night shirts changed with the fashion, but characteristic of them is a short basque, or skirt, knit back and forth in a different pattern so that the basque had side slits. The body is knit in rounds with new patterns to mark the side seams, the shoulder seams and where the body and sleeves meet. When increasing is required, it is done on either side of the vertical, dividing pattern.

Two patterns used to join the front and back.

The model shown is a roughly knit, loose-fitting short smock with three-quarter length, straight sleeves. It is knit in rounds with firmly twisted yarn, and the neckline is edged with silk tape.

The checkerboard pattern in the borders is identical on both the right and the wrong sides so that the sleeves can be worn turned up.

After the border, knit 20 rows before you begin the rounds of the star pattern. Divide the knitting into four equal parts and mark the sides, the center front and the center back. Start each round with purl 1, knit 1 (one-half of the side seam pattern). At center front, make sure that the middle stitch of the star repeat is exactly halfway between the sides. Knit the second side seam pattern: k 1, p 2, k 1. End each round with k 1, p 1 (the second half of the first side seam pattern).

Knit until the body reaches the desired length from the lower edge to the shoulder seam. (The armhole and the neck opening are cut later).

Place the front and back shoulder stitches on two separate lengths of strong yarn. Press lightly with an iron, remove the lengths of yarn, and sew the shoulder seams. (See page 34). Mark the length of the armholes and fasten the stitches on a sewing machine. Fasten the stitches around the neckline in the same manner. Then cut the openings for the armholes and the neck. Mount the sleeves and sew bias tape around the neckline.

Star repeat: A motif that was known as far back as the Renaissance. This pattern is from a book printed in Cologne in 1521.

42

Repetitive border design.

Suggested ways to increase vertical purl stitch motif. The slashes indicate increases made by using the strand of yarn between two stitches. The horizontal arrows indicate that two stitches are crossed, in other words, the second stitch is knit before the first.

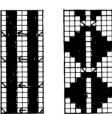

43

Shirts with horizontal stripes

Designs with horizontal stripes have always been popular. The possibilities for variation are numerous, in color and the width of the stripes as well as in the relationship between them.

In Denmark, around the middle of the last century, the farmhands' sweaters usually had narrow stripes, blue and white or red and white. The Faroese fishermen wore light blue and white undershirts with a small design in the stripes, alternately negative and positive. The beautiful "Fana" sweater from the west coast of Norway, with a star pattern across the shoulders and a checkerboard motif at the bottom is related in design to the oldest damask sweaters.

Blue and white striped knitted sleeves were often sewn onto a waistcoat of homespun. The loose sleeves could easily be replaced when they were worn out.

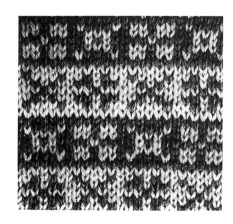

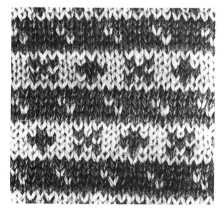

When you knit horizontal stripes in rounds, the rows will look staggered unless you knit the first stitch of each new stripe with two strands of yarn, one of each color. When you have knit the first row of the new stripe and the stitch of double yarn, carefully tighten the yarn that you wish to cover.

The old Faroese fishermen's undershirts went out of favor long ago, but the small patterns characteristic of these undershirts are still used in all the Nordic countries. (From master tailor Hans Debe's record of old, surviving patterns from the Faroe Islands).

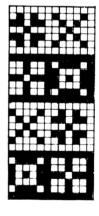

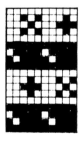

44

Shoulder pattern.

Norwegian "Fana" sweater pattern.

Two striped sweaters for children

These two small sweaters are typical of Danish and Norwegian farmers' sweaters, common during the last century.

The stripes in the "Danish" sweater are two rows wide. The only variation from the stripes is the checkerboard pattern at the cuffs and on the shoulders. The shoulder pattern appears to be different, however, simply because it contains fewer rows. The neck opening of each sweater has a folded edge, using one row of purl stitches to sharpen the hemline. The inside of the neck hem is in stockinette stitch and has no pattern.

The edges of the "Norwegian" sweater are knit with the star motif from the Norwegian "Fana" sweater. The stripes are wider and the small dots in the stripes have an added quality: they make the knitting firmer. Additionally, the dots shorten the distance between each change of color.

Checkerboard border is knit last and only on the front side.

45

"The flax is broken." In the old photograph from Odsherred in Northern Zealand, you see the typically striped farmhands' undershirts. (The end of the 19th century).

Compare the measurements of the two knitting samples, both knit with the same type of yarn and same size of needles, and see how much firmer the knitting becomes when knit with two colors on the same row, as in the Norwegian sweater to the left.

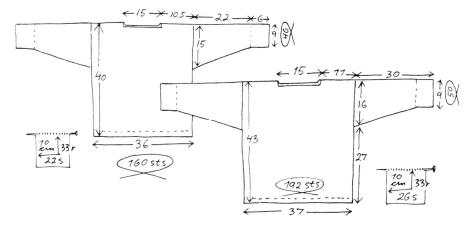

Three old patterned sweaters with common roots

The original combination of stripes and stars and the checkered border at the bottom stems from the famous Norwegian Fana sweater, named after the region. Notice the cut front, edged with woven border tape.

On Sejrø Island they knit a blue and white star pattern. The sweater has been repaired just above the lower edge by knitting with a thicker yarn – it was a real everyday sweater. According to the "tradition" there are no intervals between the checkerboard pattern and the star pattern. See also pages 17 and 61.

Woollen sweater from Halland in Sweden, knit in red and black. The detail with the initials and year is a good idea!

Notice the patterned dividing borders. The same arrangement of the sweater's net pattern is used in the sweater on page 48.

Coarse sweaters – the Icelander

"Icelander" is the old name for the sweater style worn by sailors and working men, knit with coarse yarn in no more than two or three of the wool's natural colors and in a very simple shape.

These sweaters needed first of all to be strong and warm, and multicolored knitting with very little space between the changes was used to meet these require-ments. The knitting lost its elasticity, but on the other hand, it almost had the character of woven cloth, a quality in itself. In some areas the sweaters used to be washed so that the wool would mat, or full.

This type of sweater was originally knit in a crude form without a thought for beauty but with only usefulness in mind. In a number of Nordic regions, as far back as the 1600s, Icelanders were produced by home industry for export pur-

Two sweaters that fit "everyone". The one in back has ordinary ribbed edges and sleeves narrowed at the cuffs. The model in front shows an old arrangement of patterns (see the sweater from Halland on the previous page): a double net that is filled out and arranged in different ways.

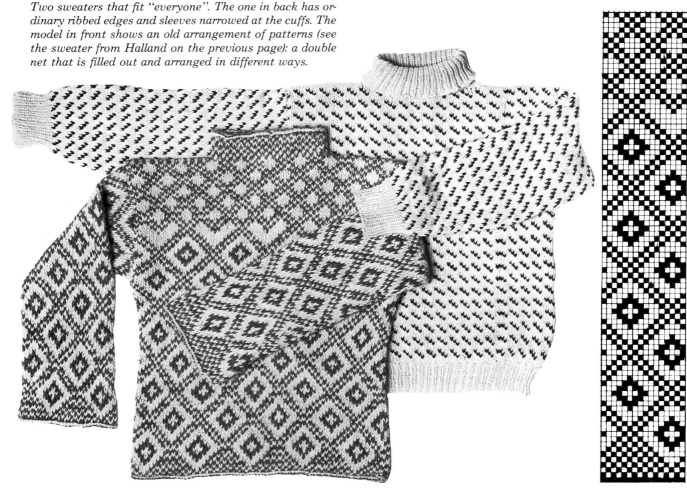

48

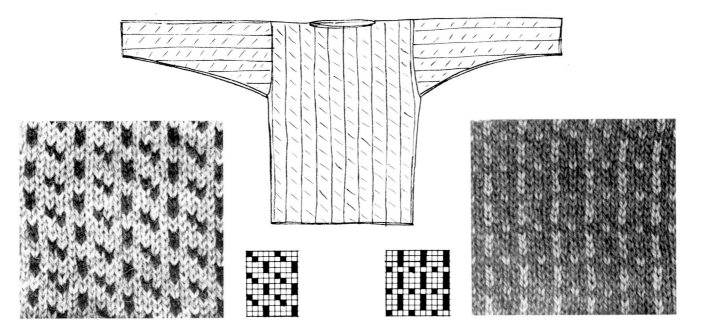

poses. The trade was so heavy that knitting was the main source of income in several areas – from the outlying Faroe Islands and Iceland to the poor moorland regions in Jutland, Denmark, and Halland, Sweden. Whole families, including the children and old people, could be found knitting.

Around the turn of the century, when interest in nature and sports began to grow, the usefulness and simple beauty of the Icelandic sweaters were discovered.

Some of the most common patterns in the sailors' sweaters were made by simply staggering the accent color. See the two samples above. The knitting tension must be the same at all times and the tension of the yarn on the wrong side is kept even.

Faroese schoolboys around 1950, wearing sweaters that show the richness and variety of the patterns found in old, everyday sweaters. Opposite are the cheap sweaters made for export. Sweaters for home use have always been knit with special care and love, and with the best quality yarn.

49

To the left is a detail showing the decreases in the sweater's sleeve and the
vertical dividing pattern.

Start first row at the * in the diagram; always knit the first stitch light
and end the row with 6 stitches of the
vertical band pattern. Each time you
decrease, knit the first row: 1st and 2nd
stitches together through the back
loop with the light yarn, so that the
light yarn lies on top of the dark loop.
At the other end of the round, decrease
by knitting the last stitch before the
light stripe together with the first
stitch of the stripe.

Instead of copying an ambitious and complicated pattern, you can find satisfaction in studying and developing the small details of a very simple pattern.

Here the slanted lines of the well-known herringbone motif have been extended at the sleeve gussets and on the sides of the body. At the lower edge of the body and the cuffs it has been further developed into rhomboid forms. At the shoulder the pattern is concluded by repeating part of the design. Yarns of choice quality make the model exclusive.

For this model, where both sleeves and body have the same edge pattern, it is necessary to start the sleeves from the wrist.

As seen in Rasmussen's sweater, you can also start a sleeve from the armhole and knit toward the wrist instead of doing the opposite. Start with the correct armhole width and knit until the sleeve is the required length.

Sweaters become jackets

When the simple farmhands' and workers' sweaters were discovered around the turn of the century and were in demand outside their own locales, the models for them were changed and refined. Children's clothes were becoming more practical and knit jackets and sweaters for children gained in popularity.

Here are two children's sweaters made with heavy Faroese yarn in symbolic patterns whose meaning is hidden from the uninitiated but is evident to any Faroese, namely the horizontal pattern, "The Seawave", and the vertical, zigzag pattern, "Sheep's Path".

The pattern is most beautiful when it is repeated all the way around the body, and is therefore unbroken by vertical, dividing patterns. When knitting the shifting pattern in "Sheep's Path", you must carefully mark the change from row to row. Both sweaters are knit according to the same measurements, but the jacket is cut up the front and edged with a ribbed band.

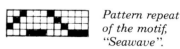

Pattern repeat of the motif, "Seawave".

Child's jacket

Knit the sleeves as described for the ordinary sweater on page 39, in this case with ribbed cuffs.

Cast the stitches for the body on a circular needle, but knit the ribbing back and forth because the

The zigzag pattern of the sweater is called "The Sheep's Path", which is not surprising to anyone who has ever seen sheep ascending a steep hillside.

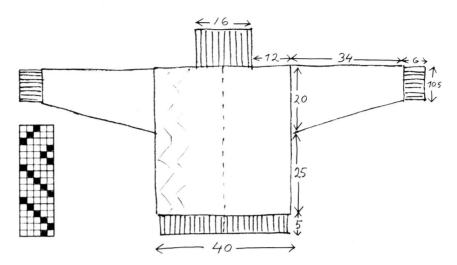

first stitches are going to be used for the vertical band. When the ribbing is finished, place the band stitches on stitch holders and start knitting in rounds.

Cast on a few extra stitches for the seams and to mark the center opening. Knit up to the shoulders and place the stitches on stitch holders or yarn ends.

Sew the shoulder seams, together (see p. 34), and attach the sleeves at the seam line.

If you knit with coarse yarn, and if the neck opening is small, you can cut the few rows down along

the mark that indicates the width of the neck, and undo the knitting to this point. The open, horizontal stitches on the front and back edges are easy to pick up as you continue knitting. The loose yarn ends of the vertical edge are sewn down on the wrong side at either side of the seam as you pick up the required number of stitches on the right side.

Reinforce the knitting with

machine-sewn stitching on either side of the center line, then cut. Rib knit the stitches placed on stitch holders for the vertical bands (one of them with buttonholes at suitable intervals) until you reach the neckline stitches. Place the vertical band stitches on the needles with the neckline stitches and rib knit the neck band. Normally a neck band is about 2 cm wide.

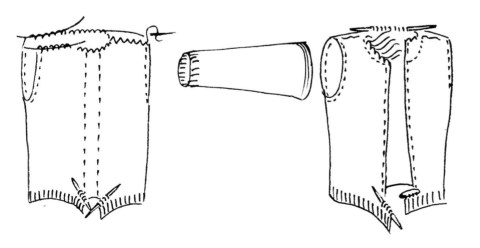

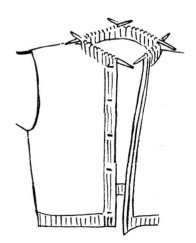

53

Moving the armhole

These drawings show how you can move the armholes deeper into the body piece to make the sweater fit tighter and to narrow the shoulders.

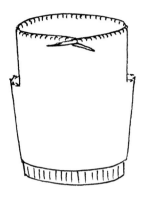

Knit up to the armhole and cast off the desired number of stitches on both sides. Knit in rounds with the remaining stitches until the knitting is the required length.

Place the neckline stitches on yarn ends, and sew or knit the shoulders together. With a double row of machine stitching, secure the knit stitches from the shoulder to the cast-off armhole stitches where the armhole seams will be. Cut.

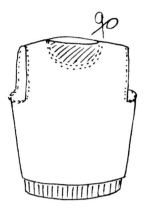

The neckline is secured with machine stitching, then cut.

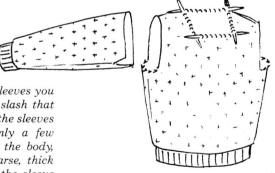

Before you can sew on the sleeves you must usually make a small slash that corresponds to the distance the sleeves are to be moved in. If only a few stitches have been cast off the body, and you have knit with coarse, thick yarn, you can just cast off the sleeve stitches loosely and stretch the knitting to fit.

The neckline stitches are picked up and the neckband or collar is knit. The machine stitching should not be visible from the right side.

The Norwegian peasant louse coat

The peasant louse coat (lusekoften) is also known as the Sete Valley sweater, as it originated in Setesdalen in Norway. Originally it was a man's sweater, part of the traditional dress of the region.

It is one of oldest of the patterned Norwegian sweaters.

The neck and sleeves were often edged with overlapping black and green cloth. In contrast to the strictly black-and-white patterns, the edges were embroidered with flowers or leaf runners, with woollen yarn in many colors.

The original peasant coat, seen below, is from the 1840s. It was "discovered" about 1930 and put into production, soon becoming a very popular tourist article.

During the German occupation of Norway, 1940-45, the sweater became a symbol of the wearer's national sentiments.

This sweater, with its wide yoke, is now considered typical sportswear and it is often knit with thicker yarn than was the original. It is knit with wool in its natural black color, in patterns that stand out as white signs between

Norwegian farmer and his son.

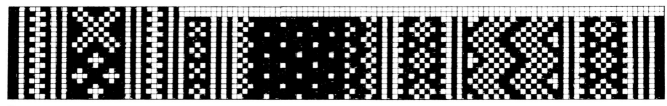

Pattern borders from the old sweater.

One of the original Norwegian peasant louse coats.

Even though it may seem odd to combine the wool with cloth edges, it is not a bad idea. The sleeves and neckline are protected, and the sweater becomes firmer.

horizontal lines on the black background.

Originally, the inspiration probably came from embroidered borders, cross-stitch patterns or designs from ancient Norwegian needlework. When these designs are knit, frequently changing color, each pattern acquires its own distinctive character. It is amazing how many different combinations you can make using these simple forms.

Seen opposite is an example of a modern sweater with a straight neck and very large armholes.

If you want a jacket with buttons and buttonholes, you can cut the sweater down the front, as described earlier, and – for example – sew on ribbed borders.

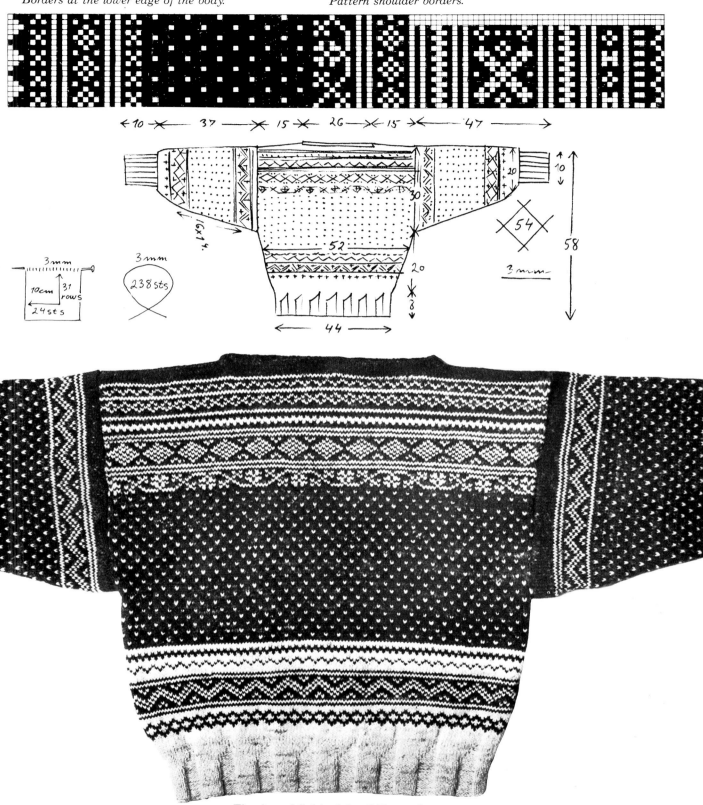

The slanted finish of the ribbing makes the change to stockinette stitch softer. A detail taken from one of the old peasant louse coats.

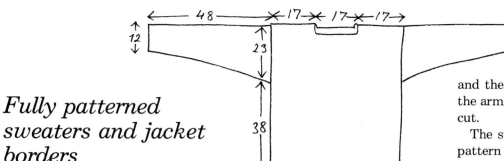

Fully patterned sweaters and jacket borders

When you want to knit a sweater with a new pattern design, it is wise to use a very simple basic pattern.

With very small details and simple techniques you can improve the fit and appearance according to your wishes and taste – for instance, change a pullover into a jacket by cutting it down the front.

Most small pattern designs will fit beautifully into any basic pattern. It is easiest to make the design and the sweater pattern compatible when you use a repeat of few stitches. If you use a repeat of a large number of stitches, make sure at least that you center the pattern at the front and back of the sweater.

The models shown are knit by following the same method as for the ordinary sweater on page 39 and the jacket on page 53, where the armholes and neck opening are cut.

The sweater with the geometric pattern is a typical everyday sweater knit with ordinary two-ply yarn. The sweater with the flower pattern is knit with a finer yarn and is somewhat fuller, so it fits as loosely as a soft fabric.

The neck opening of the geometric sweater is cut and edged with bias tape as is the Norwegian peasant louse coat. To prevent the lower edge from rippling, a narrow ribbing has been knit, turned up on the wrong side, and sewn like an ordinary hem.

A sweater can hardly be worn out if you knit with a good quality yarn. Therefore, it is advisable to use a simple, timeless, basic pattern.

A copy of an old sweater from Iveland in Norway. Notice the beautiful details on the borders and the gussets at the neck.

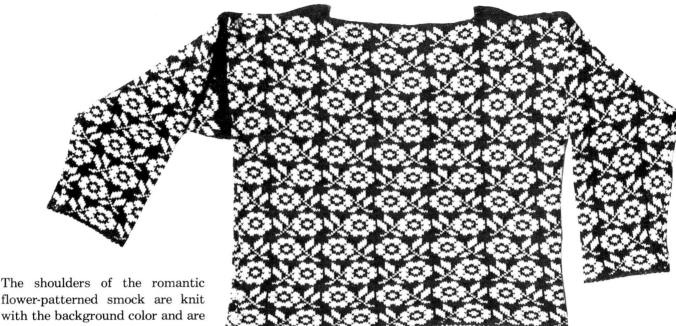

The shoulders of the romantic flower-patterned smock are knit with the background color and are slanted – partly to end the pattern repeat and partly to make the neck opening fit well. The first row of the neck opening is purled to make a sharp edge for an inside hem of stockinette stitches. The sleeves also are finished with the background color so as not to break the pattern. The cuffs of the sleeves and the lower edge of the body are also folded up, but if you prefer, you can gather the wide form with a visible ribbing.

The little child's jacket is cut down the front and stitches are gathered on to a circular needle all the way around as shown in the illustration. Work in stockinette stitch with the wrong side out so the edge will roll. Knit buttonholes on one front piece: cast off two stitches on one row and increase

two stitches at the same place on the next row. Add a few stitches at every corner, and knit a couple of stitches together in the neck opening to form it.

The child's jacket is knit with a light, irregularly spun yarn and with rather thick needles to create a soft fabric.

Formerly the Faroese women's sweaters, used for special occasions, could be knit with up to four colors in one pattern. In this small jacket one of these patterns is used. Notice that three colors are used on one row and two colors alternately on the rest of the rows. A pattern like this was normally used only for a special garment.

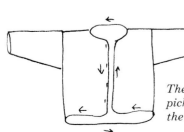

The arrows show how to pick up stitches for the edge.

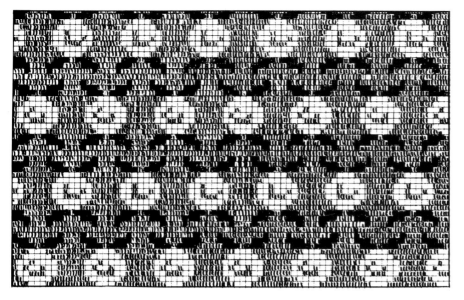

Old patterns collected from different places in the Nordic countries

Many border designs can be repeated and used as overall patterns. The example shown is a simple flowered border from a mitten from Gotland.

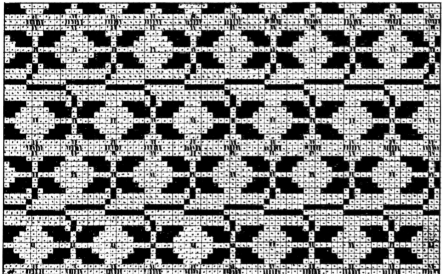

Another border design from Gotland is this leaf runner motif.

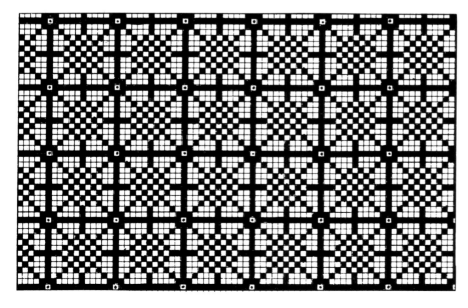

A teacher from Gotland, Hermanna Stengaard (1861–1941), collected and wrote down patterns from old fishermen's and farmers' sweaters. This old "Sunwheel" design is also from Gotland.

Here the Sunwheel has been changed a bit and now looks more like a flower. The staggering of the design neutralizes the geometric effect and makes it more romantic. The little dots in the centers of the flowers can be knit with another color or with thicker yarn to make them more lively and to join the patterns.

The star is framed in a double net, where the threads are gathered on the wrong side. This pattern form is repeated in countless variations. It is impossible to say how old a certain design is, or how and why it has become especially popular in a particular district. This pattern is found both in Finland and Estonia!

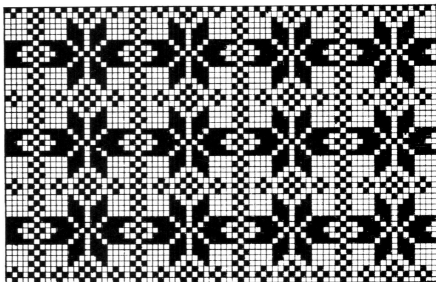

Design from the old Danish fishermen's sweater from Sejrø Island, seen on page 47.

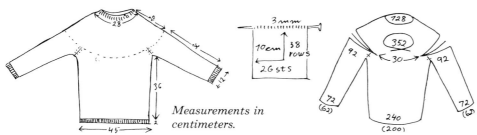

Measurements in centimeters.

Taking measurements with the number of stitches. The number in parenthesis stands for the number of stitches in the ribbing.

Raglan shape with yoke patterns

The picture of the Buxtehude Madonna, seen on page 37, shows that she is knitting the sleeves and body of a garment in one piece. This is a way of softening the shoulder line and avoiding seams, because only knitting is used.

The decreases can be placed in four slanted lines from the armhole to the neck opening, as in an ordinary raglan shape, or they can be spread evenly across the shoulders and chest. The two methods can also be combined.

This technique invites the use of traditional Nordic multicolored knitting, as the patterns help to keep track of the decreases.

Sleeves and body

Knit the sleeves and body up to the armholes according to the measurements. Place 12 stitches from the underside of each sleeve on stitch holders, 6 stitches from the end and 6 stitches from the beginning of the row. Place 12 stitches from each side of the body piece on stitch holders as well: 6 stitches from either side of both side seams. These stitches form the underside of the armhole and are finally knit or sewn together.

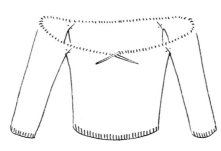

The drawing above shows how the sleeve and body stitches are gathered on a large, circular needle except for those that make up 4 centimeters of the undersides of the sleeves and the sides of the body.

To make the back slightly longer than the front, you can knit back and forth before and after the yoke pattern, leaving the front stitches unknit. This will help to place the neck opening correctly and make the sweater fit better.

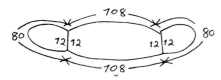

The number of stitches when the sleeves and body are joined.

The yoke

The remaining stitches of the sleeves and body are gathered on a large circular needle.

Knit 4 rounds, decreasing for the raglan sleeves on the 4th round. Place the decreases 2 stitches before and after the four gathering points.

Before starting the yoke pattern, knit a few rows back and forth on the back in order to make the neck opening lower at the front and to avoid interfering with the regularity of the pattern. Continue decreasing for the raglan sleeves and the body, 3 times altogether, over 12 rounds.

Knit until the front is 30 stitches wide, turn the knitting over, wrap the yarn once around the needle and purl to the other end of the center 30 stitches. Turn over the knitting, wrap round, and knit back.

Continue knitting and turning in this manner; however, turn the

The shape of the yoke can be compared to a truncated cone.

The cone can be divided into larger or smaller pieces with each piece corresponding to a pattern repeat. The yoke of the model shown is divided into 16 pieces and has a star pattern with 22 stitches at the bottom.

knitting for each new row on the right side of the work 8,7,6,5, and 4 stitches before the previous turn.

Knit one complete round after the last turn. Join two stitches at every turn opening to close the gaps.

After you have adjusted the number of stitches to fit the number of pattern repeats, you can begin the yoke pattern. In this case, there are 16 repeats of 22 stitches each, 352 stitches all told.

Knit the first star repeat as shown on the chart. After this, the pattern is decreased by 2 stitches, which means that every 10th and 11th stitch should be knit together.

When the narrow band pattern is finished, every 9th and 10th stitch should be joined, and so on. Every time you start a new round of decreases, there will be one stitch less between the decreases, until you have 128 stitches left (decrease 8 stitches per round, 16

times). Then knit the ribbed neck band and cast off loosely.

Finishing

The only seams in this model are made with the open stitches at the armholes. These stitches can be joined either by sewing (see page 34) or by knitting them together and casting off at the same time (see page 40).

Individual fitting

When the top of the yoke pattern has been completed, you can easily replace the circular needle with a long, strong strand of yarn and try the sweater on. The last decreases can be corrected afterward, for instance, by knitting an extra narrow border design.

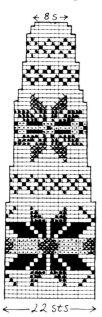

In the 1940s sweaters with patterned yokes were popular, obviously inspired by the Greenlandic beaded yoke collars. The Danish Royal Family's visit to Greenland in 1952 helped to keep this fashion alive.

Delicate blouses with lace knitting

Joining, or seaming, the different pieces of knitting is what always causes problems - not only aesthetically but also technically. It is uncomfortable in every way to wear thick and clumsy seams, and the tighter the blouse fits, the looser the seams should feel.

Described below are two blouses, where "lightness" is of greatest importance. Additionally, the use of lace knitting emphasizes this lightness.

The sleeves and body of one of the blouses are joined by crocheting (which gives a decorative effect), and the increases on the underside of the sleeves are knit like openwork, which shows how the sleeve is made.

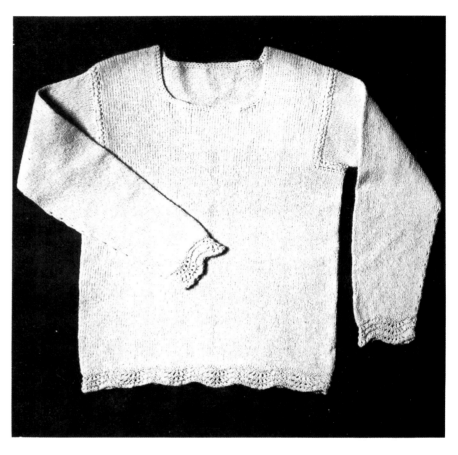

Blouse with lace borders and sleeves joined by crocheting
Body

You can begin either by knitting the borders or by casting on with waste yarn, (which will be removed when the blouse is finished) so that the borders can be knit from the open stitches. In this case the latter method is used; the advantage is that you can adjust the length of the blouse and knit the borders at the same time.

The body is knit in rounds, in stockinette stitch, up to the arm-

holes, which are 12 stitches wide on either side of the side seam mark (24 stitches for each armhole). From this point, the front and back pieces are worked separately on two needles.

When the front measures 42 cm, the neck is shaped: cast off the center 20 stitches, then on the following 3 rows: cast off 5 stitches on each side of the first row, and 1 stitch at each side of the next 2 rows.

Knit until the armhole measures

18 cm. Then cast off the shoulder stitches, slanting the shoulders up toward the neck.

First and second rows: knit two-thirds of the stitches, turn the knitting over, slip 1 stitch onto the right needle, and purl back. Third and fourth rows: knit one-third of all the stitches, turn the knitting over, slip one stitch onto the right needle, and purl back.

Fifth and sixth rows: knit all stitches. As you pick up a stitch between every turn, knit this

The use of a simple smock shape makes it possible to play with multiple color changes and stripe effects.

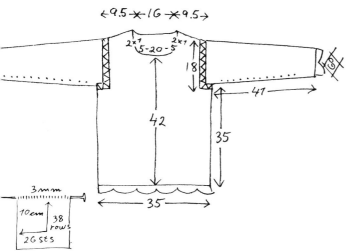

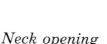

stitch and the following stitch together to avoid gaps.

Break off the yarn and knit 3 rows with waste yarn. When the shoulder pieces are finished, press the knitting carefully and remove the waste yarn. Join the shoulders by sewing them together as described on page 34.

The sleeves

Cast on with waste yarn, which will be removed when you knit the borders. Knit in rounds as you increase 2 stitches per round 12 times, that is, one stitch on either side of each change between the rounds. The increases are visible holes, because they are made simply by wrapping the yarn round the needle, and knitting it as a normal knit stitch on the following round. When the sleeve measures 41 cm, change to two needles and knit the last 16 rows back and forth to make an opening underneath the sleeve where it will be joined to the armhole. Cast off and break the yarn.

A thin yarn makes a very distinct lace-knit pattern. The blouses to the right are knit like the Aunt Anna blouse, shown on pages 68-70.

Neck opening

From the right side of the blouse, work one round of double crochet stitches, turn the work and crochet one round back to the start.

Lace border

The lace borders now can be knit at the cuffs of the sleeves and the lower edge of the body. First remove the waste yarn from the body stitches and slip them onto a circular needle. Place the sleeve stitches on four double-pointed needles. Then knit the pattern as shown on the diagram.

Alternately work six eyelets followed by six decreases on the first round. Work the following two rounds in knit stitch and purl the fourth round. Repeat these four rounds three times and cast off.

Joining the sleeves and body by crocheting

Alternate between one crochet slip stitch and one double crochet stitch, making small loops at the armhole edge and sleeve edge. Make sure that there is an equal number of loops on both pieces.

Now join the sleeve and the body by inserting the needle through the top of the first loop on the sleeve and drawing the yarn through. Then insert the needle through the top of the opposite loop on the armhole, drawing the yarn all the way through the loop of the armhole and the loop on the hook. Continue in this way by working zigzag from the sleeve to the armhole and back.

Key to symbols
V = 1 knit stitch
∩ = 1 purl stitch
O = wrap yarn around needle
◢ = 2 stitches together
◣ = 2 stitches together through back of loop

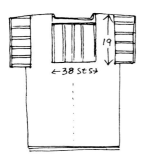

```
4.  VV  ....... ∩VV∩VV
    ∩∩  ....... V∩∩V∩∩  3.
2.  VV  ....... ∩V∩∩V
    ∩∩  ....... ◢o o◣∩∩  1.
        ← 6 sts →
```

The center 38 stitches on the front are knit according to the repeats shown.

A blouse with openwork sleeves and front piece

The simple model described on the previous pages can be changed easily, and short or long sleeves and a front pattern can be added.

The sleeves can be lace knit or openwork. To avoid seams where the body and sleeves are joined, you can pick up stitches from the body to knit the sleeves.

A small pattern can be knit on the front piece after the shoulders are finished. At that point it is easy to insert a piece of the desired size.

Whole sleeves can be knit effectively with openwork.

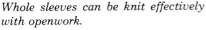

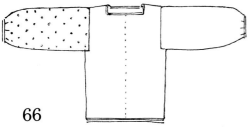

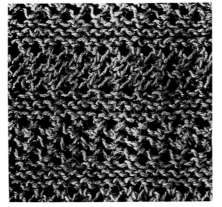

The two designs in this knitting sample can be used for the sleeves and the front piece pattern; the same simple technique is used for both: wrap the yarn around round the needle once, then purl two stitches together. First pattern: the wrapped loop is joined with the following stitch on the second row. Second pattern: the knit stitch is joined with the following wrapped loop on the second row. The patterns are worked over six rows, interrupted by six rows of knit stitches. A small variation with a tremendous effect!

```
2.  o ⃰o ⃰o ⃰
    ⃰o ⃰o ⃰o  1.

2.  V o ⃰o ⃰V
    ⃰o ⃰o ⃰o  1.
```

66

Large eyelets

Eyelets can be knit as large as you wish, as long as the number of wrapped loops is the same as the joined stitches. In this case, 4 stitches are joined to 1 stitch by slipping two stitches onto the right needle, knitting the following two together, and then slipping the two slipped stitches across the joined stitches. This decrease is followed by wrapping the yarn round the needle three times. On the following purled row, these stitches are worked as 1 purl stitch, 1 knit stitch, 1 purl stitch.

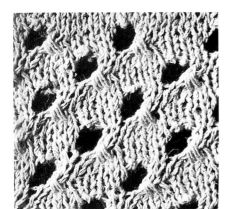

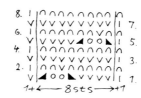

Small eyelets

In this case the eyelets are made with two wrapped loops with decreases before and after. Purling the wrapped loops on the second row gives the eyelet a special character. Compare this with the vertical openwork pattern of the front piece design.

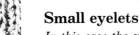

Openwork pattern

Here 3 stitches are joined to 1 stitch by slipping one stitch onto the right needle, knitting two stitches together, and then carrying the slipped stitch across the joined stitches. To restore the correct number of stitches, a wrapped loop is made on either side of the decrease. If the design is staggered every other row instead of every fourth row, as in the previous patterns, you achieve a simple lace pattern.

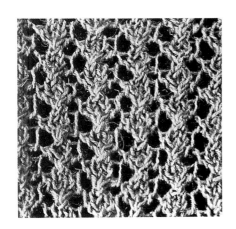

Key to symbols

| = slip 1 stitch
V = 1 knit stitch
∩ = 1 purl stitch
O = wrap yarn around needle
⋒ = 2 purl stitches together
◢ = 2 stitches together

◤ = 2 stitches together through back of loop
◺³ = slip 1 stitch, 2 stitches together, the slipped stitch across the joined stitches

◥⁴ = 2 slip stitches, 2 stitches together, the slipped stitches across the joined stitches

Instead of pattern books, old knitted borders were used as knitting samples.

Aunt Anna blouses

Once you have become familiar with the principle of the Aunt Anna blouse, you will be able to knit blouses to fit all sizes, simply by making a few changes. The sides of this sweater have distinct side stitches, which determine the measurements and the number of stitches on the sleeves and the neck opening.

The measurements of this model are given in centimeters; when the number of stitches is given, it is to show the method clearly.

Baby blouse

The materials required are approximately 150 grams of coarse cotton yarn, two knitting needles, size 2.5 mm, and one crochet hook size 1.5 mm.

The body is knit horizontally, as a band around the body. The sleeves, the collar, and the small basque are knit with stitches picked up from the body.

This little model is from the 1880s; for generations it has been knit for children in the same Copenhagen family. The original blouse was knit with unbleached cotton yarn. It had cloth buttons, and was buttoned down the back.

The sweater is worked in garter stitch, and to make a distinct side stitch edge, the last stitch of every row is slipped purlwise onto the right needle from right to left, carrying the yarn in front of the work. The first stitch of the following row is knit through the backs of the loops.

Cast on the number of stitches needed to measure 16 cm and knit 10 cm before starting the first armhole. When you reach the shoulder seam, change to waste yarn (a strong, smooth yarn that can be removed afterward). With this

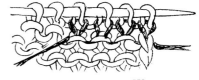

Waste yarn

yarn knit 7 cm (18 stitches) on a short stocking needle. Break the yarn and change back to the blouse yarn and the blouse needles. Continue working in garter stitch until you have knit 20 cm from the armhole. Then knit the second armhole like the first one, followed by 10 more centimeters, and cast off.

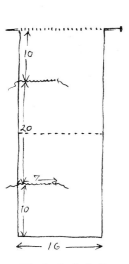

The body is knit in one piece.

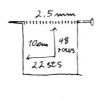

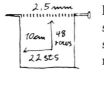

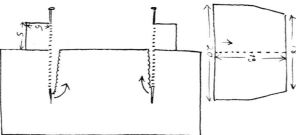

Picking up stitches for the sleeves.

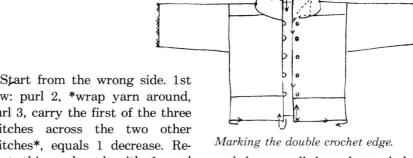

Marking the double crochet edge.

Side stitch edge.

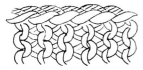

Pick up one stitch through the back of the loop of every shoulder stitch, that is 11 stitches on both sides. (From the front put the left needle into the back of the loop and knit the stitch twisted onto the right needle). Knit 22 rows (5 cm) and cast off. Slip the first stitch onto the right needle as before and knit the first stitch through the back of the loop. When both shoulder pieces have been knit, press the work, and remove the waste yarn. After these loose stitches have been picked up from the armholes and the shoulder pieces (in all, 11 stitches plus 18 stitches plus 18 stitches, or 47 stitches), knit the sleeves until they measure 13 cm and have a couple of decreases along the sides. Cast off and break the yarn.

The neck opening

Pick up stitches all along the neck opening (still working through the backs of the loops, knitting the stitches twisted on the needle). Knit five rows of stockinette stitch followed by three rows of eyelet (openwork knitting). Make sure that the total number of stitches is a multiple of three, plus three edge stitches.

Start from the wrong side. 1st row: purl 2, *wrap yarn around, purl 3, carry the first of the three stitches across the two other stitches*, equals 1 decrease. Repeat this and end with 1 purl stitch. 2nd row: knit all stitches. 3rd row: purl 1 stitch,* purl 3 stitches, carry the first stitches across the two other stitches and wrap the yarn around the needle*. Repeat this and end with 2 purl stitches. 4th row: knit as 2nd row. 5th row: knit as 1st row. Work five rows in garter stitch and cast off on the 5th row.

Bottom edge, the basque

Pick up stitches as for the neck opening, and knit five rows of garter stitch, five rows of eyelet, five rows of garter stitch again, and cast off.

The blouse is edged all the way around with a crocheted border and has small loop buttonholes down the front.

Double crochet one row from the bottom of the left side up to the neck opening and fasten the yarn. Then work one row of double crochet starting from the bottom of the right up toward the neck opening, and another row back. On the return row make five loop buttonholes with crocheted slip stitches.

Around the neck opening crochet a picot edge: 3 double crochet stitches, 2 slip stitches that are worked through the loop of the last double crochet loop, etc. When you reach the left side of the blouse, work a double crochet edge again and continue the picot border around the bottom.

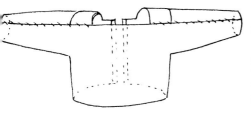

The diagram shows how the sleeves are folded toward the back and sewn so that the seam is level with the shoulder piece. The sleeves must be joined to the body by sewing through the back of each loop in order to obtain an edge as distinct as the side seam edge.

69

2. V V   V V V V
    O ◣³ O V V V   1.
    ← 6 sts →

The Aunt Anna blouse for adults

The model shown is knit with thin, light yarn and it weighs approximately 250 grams.

To figure out how many stitches the body requires – length and height – it is advisable to knit a small gauge swatch with the yarn you plan to use. Then you can follow the diagram, modifying it to suit your own measurements and wishes. Unlike the child's blouse, this blouse has a shaped body with darts made by turning the rows before they are ended. The basque is knit in the same direction as the body but separately, so that it is possible to adjust the length along the way. The openwork pattern has a vertical effect, just as the shoulder pattern has.

A plain row of eyelet is knit between the sleeves and the body to emphasize the transition from the sleeves to the body. The eyelet at the bottom of the sleeves can be used with a string woven through it to gather the sleeves at the wrist.

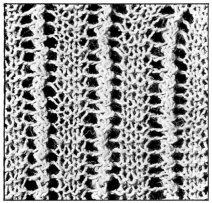

2nd row: k all stitches. Repeat these two rows until the pattern is as long as you wish.

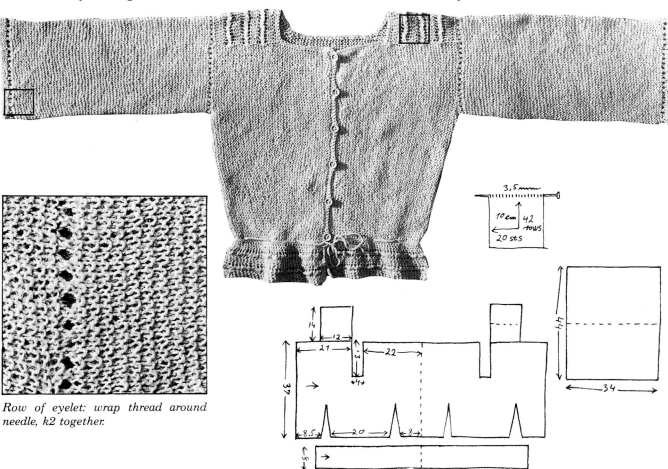

Row of eyelet: wrap thread around needle, k2 together.

70

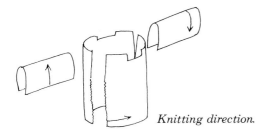

Knitting direction.

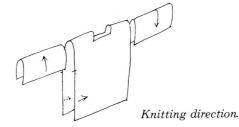

Knitting direction.

Two fulled smocks

To make the vertical colored stripes in this blouse, the body and the sleeves are knit in vertical rows. Then, to further emphasize the stripes, the stockinette stitch work is turned wrong side out.

The most simple model has been used to make these two smocks, and the possible color combinations are endless for both the smaller and the larger size. To blend the colors and the material, they are fulled afterward. The simple pattern is well suited to fulling, which is described in detail on page 124. Finally, the smock can be made to fit all different sizes and shapes simply by taking in the few seams or letting them out.

Before you begin, take the important measurements: the chest, the desired length, and the distance from one wrist to the other across the back. Rough, standard measurements are shown on the two diagrams below; remember, however, that a fulled garment will contract, so do not forget to make a fulled sample!

Materials

Many shades of colors have been used in the two examples, and the knitting yarn is a two-ply, rather firmly twisted weaving yarn (the same quality as one would use for a woven blanket). For an adult sweater approximately 500 grams of yarn are needed. If you use needles of size 2.5 mm and full the sweater lightly after knitting it, 10 cm will amount to 25 stitches and 35 rows.

Choosing colors

The body and the sleeves of both smocks are divided into three parts, separated by narrow stripes. The distribution of the colors in the child's smock is seen below, as an example: two blue colors that have the same relative strength are used for the wide stripes, A and B. For instance, blue green, aquamarine or royal blue.

Narrow stripes often tend to fuse into one color when seen from a distance. They can be either light or dark, strong or weak, and this is why the narrow stripes of C are composed of bright colors. The stripes down the sides are neutral.

The symmetrical basic division of the stripes can be broken down and built up again by reversing the narrow stripes on the front and back.

Child's smock
Body

First cast on 190 stitches with waste yarn, then work the number of rows given below using the colors of your choice. Knit so that most of the color changes are made at the back. Mark the center of the 190 stitches, so you can calculate the neck opening a bit lower at the front than at the back. Cast off the 12 stitches of the neck opening. At the same time you should mark the armholes 31 stitches to either side of the center.

After having cast off one side of the neck opening, work the front and back separately. At this point, the narrow groups of stripes, C and D, should be reversed to contrapose the colors on the front and back. When the neck opening has been completed, cast on 12 new stitches for the other shoulder and knit the second part of the smock. Finally, when all rows have been knit, complete the body with 4 rows of waste yarn. Remember to mark the armhole on this side, too.

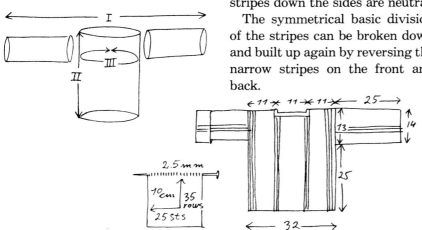

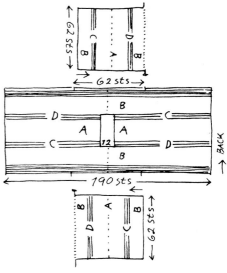

71

The sleeves

The change of color is done so that all loose ends are at the seam where the sleeve joins the body.

The number of stitches and rows are shown on the diagrams of the two smock sizes (one on page 71 and one on page 72). Notice that the groups of narrow stripes, C and D, are reversed from the front to the back on the second sleeve of the child's smock, because both sleeves are knit alike!

When all rows are knit, cast off the stitches and sew the sleeves together.

Adult smock

Body

To avoid having too many stitches on the needles at one time, knit the front and back separately and sew them together at the shoulders and on the right side.

The smock in the diagram to the right has narrow stripes to divide the colors – the ones down the center are 2 rows wide and the ones down the sides are 4 rows wide. In this case, the wide stripes can be divided into smaller sections with even more colors, but notice that the stripes will continue from the front over the shoulders and down the back when the shoulder seams are joined.

The adult smock is knit in the same way as the child's smock. The yarn ends should all be fastened at the armholes of the sleeves and at the lower edge of the body. The sleeves are knit like the sleeves of the child's smock.

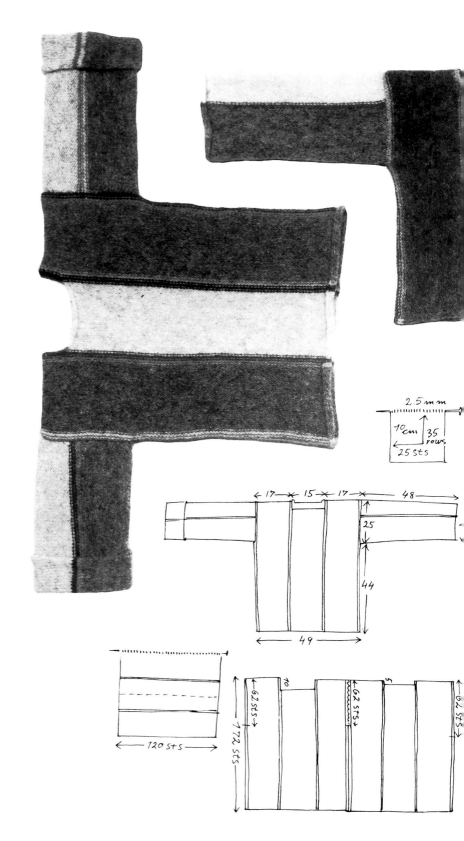

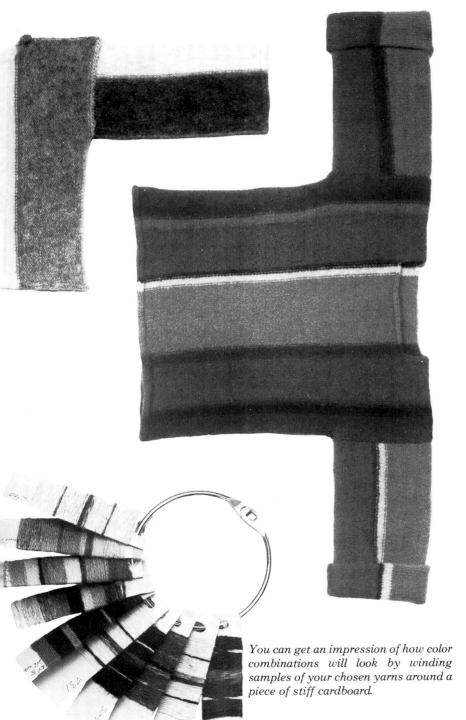

Finishing

All the yarn ends should be fastened by sewing them through stitches of their own color.

Lightly press the part worked in waste yarn to stabilize the stitches. Remove the waste yarn, pick up the armhole stitches and cast them off as usual. Do not cast off too loosely. Stitch the remaining side stitches (see page 34). The sleeves should be joined to the body using a back stitch.

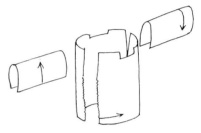

It is unnecessary to hem the lower edge or the sleeves, or to edge the neckline of this simple smock.

The carefully finished smock, with its invisible side seam stitches and hidden yarn end fastenings, should not be defaced by heavy edgings. Let the smock remain simple.

You can get an impression of how color combinations will look by winding samples of your chosen yarns around a piece of stiff cardboard.

Try to make the number of windings proportionate to the number of rows you are going to knit of each color. This is how weavers always have made stripe samples!

73

Shawls and scarves

In the last century large shawls or scarves, oblong or triangular, were often used as outdoor clothing. It was common at that time to knit shawls in garter stitch so the fabric would be the same on both sides.

There are many possibilities for variation using garter stitch. You should merely be aware of techniques like visible or invisible decreasing and increasing, for example, and of the placement of the elements that shape the fabric. Then you can give the knitting decorative features.

Unlike the traditional shawls from the Shetland Islands, which are square and have beautiful lace-knit patterns, the Nordic shawls are usually three-cornered in shape and are very simply made. Usefulness was emphasized more than the decoration.

Garter stitch triangular shawl. Basic form I

Cast on 1 stitch, and knit 1 stitch through back of loop and 1 stitch through front of loop, turn over. Slip the first stitch of the 2nd row onto the needle, and knit 1 stitch through back of loop and one stitch through front of loop as before; turn over. Continue in this way for the rest of the rows by slipping the first stitch onto the needle and knitting two stitches through the last stitch of the row; the middle stitches should be knit in the ordinary manner.

The easiest way to make a triangular shape is to start with one stitch and then increase with one stitch on each row until the shawl is the desired size.

The diagram above shows the simple design in which any combination of colors can be used. Here you can see how the soft rounding of the long edge makes the shawl fit well.

To make the top of the shawl slightly rounded, you can work in turned rows on the last part.

When you have not quite reached the center of the shawl, turn the knitting over, slip the first stitch onto the right needle, and knit to the edge as usual. The following row should be turned just before you reach the center. Until the top of the shawl is rounded suitably, you should continue turning the rows further and further away from the center every time. The stitches should all be cast off on one row, and you should decide whether you want the edge tight or loose.

You can knit the shawl the other way around, that is, by casting on the number of stitches you want at the longest edge, and decreasing along the sides until there is only one stitch left.

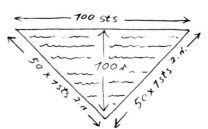

Triangular shawl. Basic form II

Cast on as many stitches as it takes to make the long edge of the shawl the desired length, and decrease where you increased before: on each row, the 1st stitch is slipped onto the needle and the last two stitches are knit together.

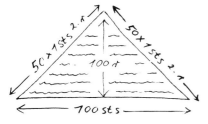

When using this method, the depth of the shawl from top to bottom will be as many rows as the number of stitches cast on. The rounded top, described in Basic form I, can also be made with this method.

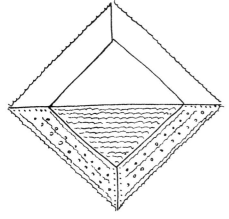

Two garter stitch triangles can be knit together to form a square. A border can be added by picking up stitches from each side separately and knitting back and forth – with a pattern, for instance. Decrease by wrapping the yarn around the needle at the beginning of each row and joining the corners when all four sides are finished.

A Faroese girl wearing a tied shawl. Notice that she is holding the knitting yarn across her right index finger.

75

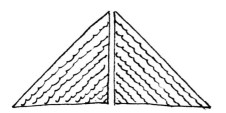

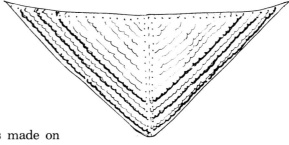

Double-triangle shawl increased from the neck. Basic form III

Two triangular shapes can be knit together to form a triangle that is double in size. The knitting direction will then follow the two short edges of the shawl.

You can start at the center of the long edge and increase, or with both short edges and decrease, according to the method you prefer and to the decorative patterns you will use.

One stitch is increased on both sides of every other row, just as in the simple basic triangle form I.

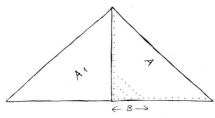

By increasing a few extra stitches spread out across the first part, marked B on the diagram, you can achieve a better fit across the shoulders.

This part, which should be about 17 or 18 cm, corresponds to one-half the width of the shoulder.

The rest of the shawl is knit without adding any stitches other than those at the beginning of each row and at the center.

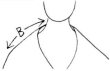

The first triangle, A, is made on the first knit row, and triangle A1 is made on the return knit row.

Cast on 3 stitches.

First row: knit 1 stitch through front of loop and 1 stitch through back of loop of the 1st stitch, wrap the yarn from behind the work around the right needle (an invisible increase is made), knit the 2 last stitches. 2nd row: knit 1 stitch through front and 1 stitch through the back of the first loop as before, wrap the yarn from behind the work across the right needle, k1 (this is the center stitch), knit the last three stitches.

Knit the remaining rows in this way, by increasing the first stitch and wrapping around the needle immediately before the center stitch.

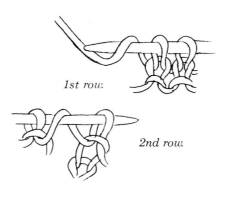

1st row.

2nd row.

Each center wrap-around stitch will remain visible until it has been knit on the return row; therefore, it marks the point for the next wrap-around at the center.

Double-triangle shawl decreased from the lower edge. Basic form IV

This basic pattern is shown in an old Norwegian knitting book "for school and home" from 1909. The shawl is formed by fitting two triangles together. This method calls for casting on the number of stitches required for the two short edges and decreasing until there is only one stitch left.

Cast on from 300 to 450 stitches, according to the yarn and size of needles, plus 1 stitch at the center; mark this with a thread. In this case, the decreases are made at the end of each row and the first two stitches after the center stitch are knit together.

On all rows: slip the first stitch onto the right needle, work until the center stitch is knit, then knit the next 2 stitches together. Knit until there are 3 stitches left and knit the first two together, then knit the last stitch.

Continue working in this way until approximately one-fifth of the original number of stitches are left; then decrease at the beginning of each row, as well, to shape the neck.

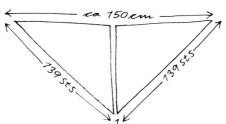

Shawl with picot casting on and patterned borders

The shawl seen on the colored pages is knit from Basic form IV. Instead of casting on in the ordinary manner, however, a picot border is used.

The yarn weight is approximately 100 grams. It is a fine wool knit with 5-6 mm needles.

Picot border

Cast on 1 stitch. Knit 1 stitch and place it back on the left needle, turned. Repeat this until there are 5 stitches on the needle (the two-needle method; see page 31). Knit 2 stitches, carry the first stitch across the second stitch (1 decrease). Knit 1 stitch and cast off as before. Repeat this until there is only 1 stitch left. One picot has now been completed. Move this picot to the left needle and knit as before.

When you have knit 139 picots, pick up 2 stitches from each picot, so that you have 278 stitches in all. One extra stitch should be knit, to obtain an uneven number of stitches to mark the center stitch.

The stitches are picked up from the right side of the work, and in this case, all the decreases are also made on the right side of the work. The decreases are made at the beginning and end of each row, 5 stitches from the edges, as well as just before and right after the center stitch. On the wrong side, all rows are knit. After eight rows, begin the first row of openwork on the wrong side of the work.

Openwork with purled eyelet

Knit the first 7 edge stitches, bring the yarn in front of the left needle, insert the right needle through the first two stitches *in front* of the yarn and purl them together. (This way, the yarn is wrapped automatically). Knit eyelet until you reach the 5 center stitches, knit them, then knit eyelet again up to the last 7 edge stitches. On the return row, which is worked with the usual decreases, knit each wrapped stitch through the back of loop. After three rows without any pattern, the next two rows are knit like long, twisted knit stitches.

Long, twisted knit stitches

Start on the right side of the work, decreasing as usual.

Bring the yarn in front of the left needle and insert the right needle through the first stitch as for a knit stitch, but lead the needle away from the yarn. Wrap the yarn around the needle, under and over, then bring the needle back as shown on the diagram. Repeat throughout the row. Knit the second row as the last row. Then knit five rows, followed by a row of eyelet as before.

Knit until you have about 60 stitches left (one-fifth the original number of stitches) and thereafter decrease more rapidly: decrease four extra stitches on every decrease row. Spread these decreases evenly over the row. Decrease in this manner until there are only 10 edge stitches left. Because the edges meet at the center, these stitches should finally be sewn or knit together.

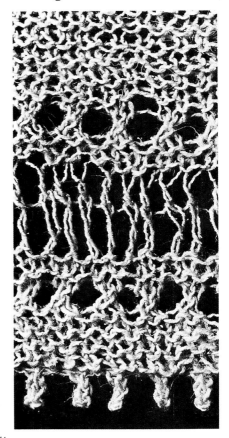

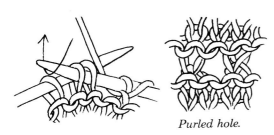

Purled hole.

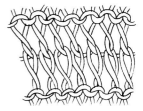

Long, twisted knit stitches.

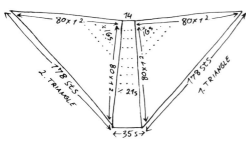

On the diagram, the total number of stitches cast on is 391 and these are divided so that each triangle has 178 and the gusset 35.

Faroese shawl

Until recent times, women of the Faroe Islands wore a type of shawl like the Norwegian school model (see page 76). To make it fit well, however, they knit a gusset down the center with decreases.

These shawls were also worked in garter stitch and often had one or more openwork borders.

After casting on, the first four rows are knit without decreasing, and sides of the center 35 stitches are marked with thread. All the decreases are made in the first half of the work, as follows.

First row: knit 8 stitches (edge stitches), 2 stitches together, knit to the first marking thread and knit 2 stitches together, knit to the end of the row. 2nd row: knit like the first row, so that both triangular shapes are decreased on every other row.

Repeat these two rows over and over. It is possible to make an openwork border after the first 20 rows. It can be about 40 rows wide.

By decreasing regularly you will gradually make the center gusset narrower. Three stitches can be decreased in one row, say, every 10th row.

The edge stitches are decreased with one stitch every 20 rows, and

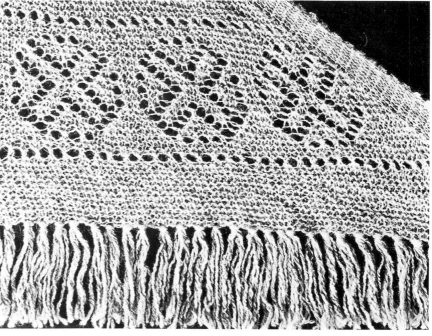

A Faroese shawl is especially beautiful when it is knit with the finest, soft "pluck" wool, wool which has been manually sorted from the coarse, top wool. This shawl weighs about 150 grams and is worked on a circular needle, using garter stitch.

the last 14 stitches of the center gusset are cast off at one time.

To round the shoulders handsomely at the top of both triangles, decrease by 16 extra stitches, marked as dots on the diagram. The first extra decreases should be made on about the 98th row – decrease eight stitches. The second extra decreases should be made on the 124th row – decrease seven stitches.

30 row

Key to symbols

- ● = wrap yarn around needle
- V = 1 knit stitch
- ◢ = knit 2 stitches together
- ◣ = knit 2 stitches together through back of loop
- ▲ = knit 3 stitches together

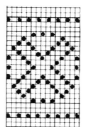

Every pattern row is followed by a knit stitch return row. For the sake of clarity these return rows have not been drawn on the chart.

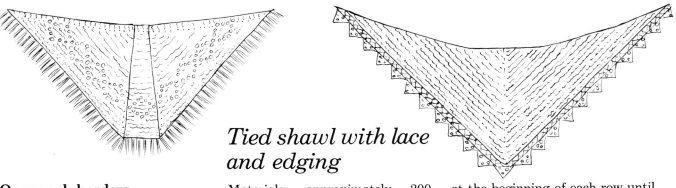

Openwork borders

Openwork patterns can be drawn on graph paper; however, you must remember that every row of eyelet consists of two rows: 1st row, the eyelet is made by wrapping the yarn around the needle and knitting two stitches together before or after the wrapping, and 2nd row, the eyelet is completed by straight purling or knitting.

A distinct vertical row of eyelet is made on every fourth row (or on every other row on the right side of the work) as described on page 22; and a slanted row of eyelet, where the eyelet is staggered, can be made on every other row of the right side of the work.

Tied shawl with lace and edging

Materials: approximately 200 grams of fairly thin, two-ply yarn and a circular needle, 6 mm.

The yarn should not be too thick for a tied shawl that is long enough to cross in the front and be tied in back. The lace edge can be knit first (see the following pages) and the stitches picked up from the side edges, whereupon the shawl is knit according to Basic form IV. Two stitches should be decreased at the beginning of each row until only two-thirds of the original number of stitches remain. Then knit 2 stitches together at the beginning of each row and at the center. In this way you can make the shawl wider without making it deeper at the same time. This model also has a softly rounded neckline, which is done towards the end by decreasing 1 extra stitch on every row, staggering it from row to row.

Once you have become familiar with the principle of pattern graphs, you'll find it easy to use drawings like the above.

The ends of an ordinary, triangular shawl can be made longer, so that the shawl can be tied behind the back.

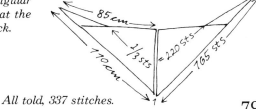

All told, 337 stitches.

Conscientious use of colors and patterns gives the knit work a very personal touch.

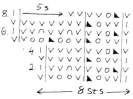

Lace and edging

A knit lace border is characterized by the wavy edge on one side and the firm, straight edge on the other side. The firm side can be used for decoration, but it is also suitable for picking up stitches. The shapes are made by increasing at the end of the row by wrapping the yarn around the needle. The decreases are made at the beginning of the row on the wrong side of the work, until the lace form is finished and the original number of stitches is restored.

The photographs at the right show three different lace borders. The lace with three rows of eyelet is used for casting on for the tied shawl.

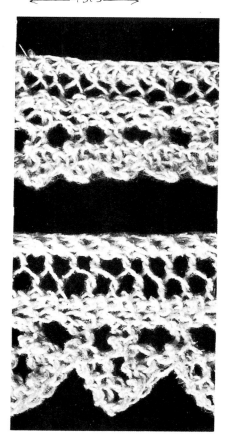

One-hole eyelet with lace edge

The vertical lines on the diagram divide the different patterns. The edge stitches are shown first and last. They are always knit: slip first stitch and knit last stitch. The first four stitches make one of the simplest lace patterns and they are worked the same on the right and wrong sides. Then an eyelet is made by wrapping the yarn twice around the needle. These wrappings are always worked: k1, p1, on the return row. The original number of stitches, 9, is restored by casting off the first 2 stitches on the 4th row.

Three-hole eyelet with lace edge

This lace border is made like the previous one-hole eyelet; however, this one has three double holes, and the jagged edge is completed with five stitches.

Border with a zigzag edge and eyelet

This border, with an openwork pattern, is knit with additions made by wrapping the yarn around the needle – but the last wrapping is not followed by knitting 2 together. The decreases start on the 10th return row, immediately after the eyelets have been finished by knitting the previous row.

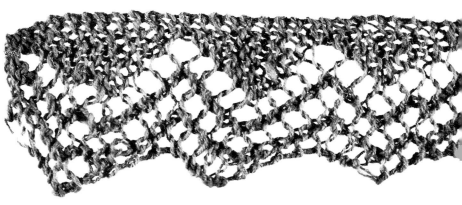

Notice that when the decreasing is begun, all the wrappings for the eyelets are followed by knitting 2 stitches together on all the unevenly numbered rows. To make the last eyelet on every row more distinct, you can wrap the yarn twice around the needle, but the double wrapping should be knit as one stitch on the return row.

Key to symbols

| = slip 1 stitch (onto the right needle)

V = 1 knit stitch

∩ = 1 purl stitch

O = wrap yarn around needle

◢ = 2 stitches together

◣ = 2 stitches together through back of loop

80

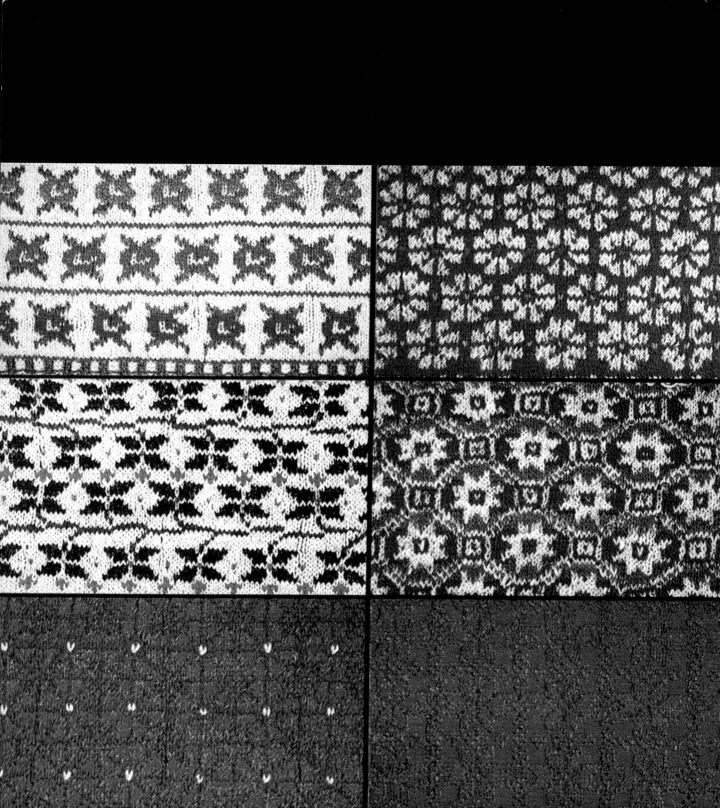

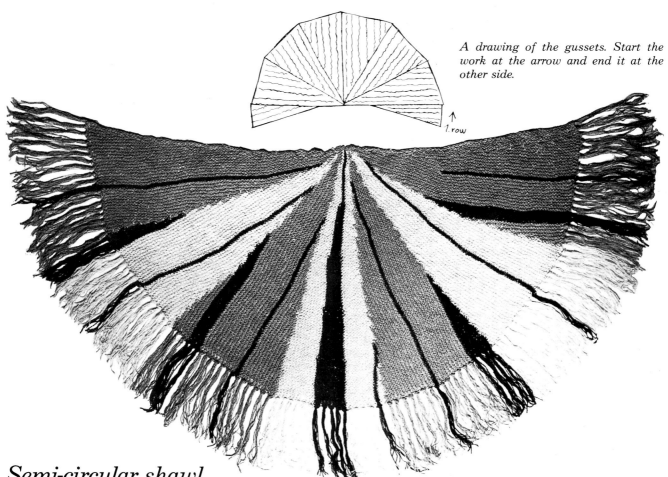

A drawing of the gussets. Start the work at the arrow and end it at the other side.

1. row

Semi-circular shawl knit with gussets

To emphasize the gussets, the model is knit with many colors. This makes it possible to add simple stripes, and to keep track of new gussets made inside the main gussets. The shawl is knit solely in garter stitch with shortened, turned rows. The first row starts at the outer edge of the shawl, and the first stitch is always slipped purl-wise onto the right needle.

Cast on 91 stitches (50 cm), not too tightly. Knit 5 stitches, turn the work over, slip the first stitch onto the needle, and knit 5 stitches back to the edge. Turn the knitting over and work as before, but this time, knit 5 stitches before turning. Continue in this way, knitting 5 more stitches each time, until 90 stitches are knit. (The 91st stitch is the center of the shawl and should never be knit).

You have now knit back and forth eighteen times and have reached the middle of the gusset. From this point on, the work is reversed, that is, 90 stitches minus 5, or 85 stitches which are knit before turning. At the next turn, 80 stitches are knit, and so on, until the last 5 stitches are knit and the gusset is finished. The second gusset is knit in the same way; however, you should stagger the turns to avoid perceptible holes. Turn the work over for the first time after the first 3 stitches, then work the gusset as before, with 5 stitches between the turns.

A shawl knit with gussets has one sensitive point: the center. It consists of 1 stitch and 7 gusset points. Every time you reach a gusset point, you pick up one stitch and knit it together with the 90th stitch. (This is best seen when you have the work in front of you).

When the shawl's seven gussets have been completed – with the change of colors and stripe effects you have chosen – cast the work off, but not too tightly, and so that the closing edge has the same firmness as the cast-on edge.

Knit samples of the patterns from pages 60-61.

Caps

The simplest cap is a stockinette stitch tube that is gathered at the top. At the bottom you can make an elastic, ribbed border, or a folded cuff, so that the edge is double. This basic form allows for endless decorative variations, and naturally, the choice of materials here is of great importance.

Cap with multi-colored border

The cap is knit in rounds, using stockinette stitch and, for example, two-ply, plant-dyed yarn which is found in many soft colors. The cap is gathered at the top and is supplied with a big pompon of many different shades of green.

The cap has an inside folded cuff, knit with needles that are one-half size thinner than the needles used for the rest of the cap. This makes the cap fit tightly. Size 2 mm needles are used. A total of 132 stitches is cast on for the inside cuff, which measures 6 cm.

Size 3 mm needles have been used to knit the multicolored part, because this technique results in tighter knitting than does plain stockinette stitch. Follow the diagram, or use one of the other pattern diagrams in the book.

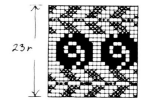

Rose motif from Gotland.

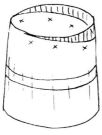

You can turn the knitting over when you have almost reached the back, and knit to a similar point on the other side of the back. The next turn should be made further toward the front – the thinner the yarn, the more turns.

You can make the cap fit better by working the top of the tube in shortened, turned rounds. In this way you can make the front longer than the back. If the cap is just a few centimeters shorter at the back, you will avoid the unpleasant feeling of the cap rubbing against your collar.

When the cap is the desired length, cast off the stitches, and gather the top, but not too tightly because you should leave room for the big pompon.

Pompon

Most people know how to make a pompon, but this one is made from two pompons and has a flat bottom.

Collect all the colors you are going to use, and wrap the yarn around a tin can, or a jar with a diameter of about 12 cm. Wrap the yarn as many times as you find

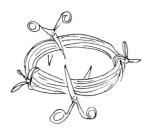

When the yarn wrapping has been tied safely at two points opposite each other, the wrapping should be cut so that one half is longer than the other.

reasonable, but remember that one wrapping becomes two pompons.

One-half is going to be the bottom. It is sewn together with chain stitches and made into a ring; the yarn sticks out in all directions, as shown on the diagram.

The other half is gathered with a back stitch seam, as seen in the diagram. Then the two pompons are sewn together by joining the two seams all the way around. The completed pompon can then be sewn onto the cap and cut to give it the right shape.

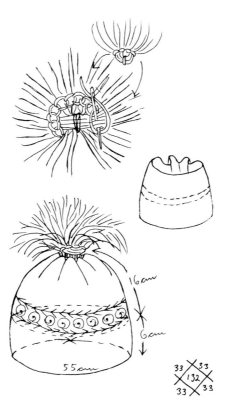

Cap with turned up, double edge

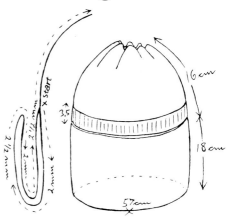

The diagram shows where and why the size of needles should be changed. You can also cast on fewer stitches and decrease and increase according to need.

The change of color marks the part of the cap which is visible after the cuff is folded and where a border could reasonably be placed, or where decoration could start.

This cap is knit in the same way as the last one, but the folded cuff is knit three times longer. It can be folded up twice, which makes it twice as warm. It can also be pulled down to cover the ears.

This cap is made with the same number of stitches as the previous one: 132 stitches. The size of needles has been changed here, too, to make the folded cuff fit well, so the outer layer is not too tight and the inner layer does not ruffle.

The cap is knit with two-ply yarn in natural colored wool in three different parts – and all the colors are gathered in the pompon.

Simple cap with multicolored knitting

This cap is based on the same simple design as the previous ones, but has no pompon or folded cuff. It is made to fit with an inside ribbed border, and multicolored knitting is used for both decoration and extra warmth. At the same time, the knitting can reflect imagination and joy in its colors.

The yarn quality is the same as for the previous two caps – rather thin, two-ply yarn – and the num-ber of stitches is somewhat greater, since the knitting is multicolored – 140 stitches in all.

The inside piece, formed by turning the edge under, is knit with 2.5 mm needles: k1, p1 in one of the pattern's contrast colors to emphasize the scalloped edge, which is knit by wrapping the yarn around the needle and knitting the next two stitches together. The following round is knit and then the yarn color is changed to the pattern's background color.

Work the multicolored knitting with the chosen colors and design until the cap measures 18 cm from the lower edge. From here, knit the shortened back, and when the front part measures 22 cm, cast off. Gather at the top as usual, but more tightly than for a cap with a pompon.

Around the turn of the century, when interest in sports and outdoor life was growing and tourist articles became an institution, naturalistic motifs, like dancing women and children, animals and birds, became popular subjects for knitting patterns.

The motifs were often taken from, or inspired by, cross-stitch patterns and were combined in many ways. They could be used as horizontal bands, as a single border or as individual figures framed by geometric patterns.

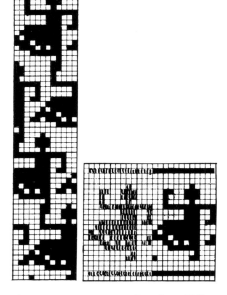

A knitting motif from The Sete Valley in Norway, "Dancing Granny", can be used as a horizontal band but can also be used staggered and chained together.

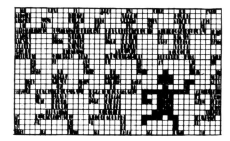

Running, playing children. By changing one simple stitch a boy in trousers can be made into a girl wearing a dress.

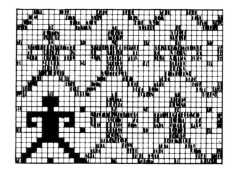

When the space between the change of colors becomes too great, the yarn should be twisted on the wrong side of the work (see page 107). You can also make a little stitch dot that does not interfere with the pattern, but fastens the yarn. See the example of the man or boy flexing his muscles.

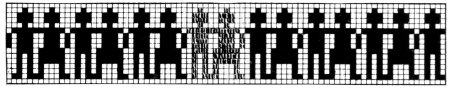

84

Cap with patterned border on the fold, and shaped crown

It can be fun to knit a patterned border on the folded cuff of a plain cap. The cuff becomes firmer, and you can experiment with simple pattern forms and the combinations of colors on this rather short piece.

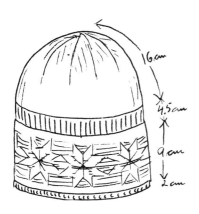

The cap model has the popular star motif as a border. After the border, a 4 to 5 cm ribbing is knit to make the inside more elastic. The advantage of the star motif is that the pattern is the same regardless of which way you knit it.

∩ = *purl*
I = *slip 1 stitch (onto the needle), carrying the yarn forward*

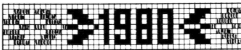

The crown

The 24 stitches on each needle are divided into three parts, so that three decreases can be made on each needle. 1st decrease round: k6, 2 together, repeat to the end of the round. Knit the same number of rounds as there are stitches between the decreases on the first round. 2nd decrease round: k5, 2 together, continue to the end of the round. Knit 5 rounds without decreasing.

On every new round of decreases, there should be 1 stitch less than on the previous round, and the same number of rounds less without decreases, until there are 12 stitches left. Break the yarn and draw it through the remaining stitches, so that you close the gap at the top. Then fasten the yarn end.

Many motifs for knit borders originally came from cross-stitch books. Dates and alphabets were also found there, but they should always be combined with band patterns that are the same width, because of the threads running along the wrong side.

 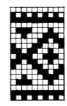

The cuff is folded in such a way that the patterned border, like this leaf runner motif, for example, should be worked from the top to the bottom.

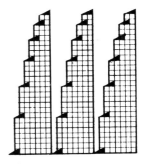

Division of 12.

▲ = *2 stitches together.*

The decreasing method shown above makes a beautifully shaped closing of a cylinder form. Whether you divide the shape into twelve parts, as done here, or ten or eight parts, depends on how elongated you want the top to be.

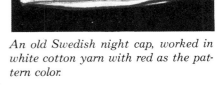

An old Swedish night cap, worked in white cotton yarn with red as the pattern color.

85

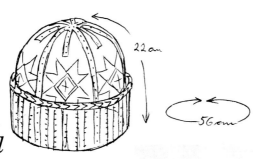

Cap with patterned crown

When you study the old patterns and their origins, now and then you come across clues as to their symbolic meanings. This used to be reason for choosing a certain pattern.

It was believed that no bodily harm would befall the person wearing a cap decorated with the ladder pattern – a symbol of Jesus' suffering, just as the star is an old Christian symbol. It might be of some comfort, to one who is just a little superstitious, to knit these symbols in a ski cap or, as shown on page 105, a pair of ski mittens.

The tale of the meaning of this pattern comes from Estonia. Here many of the knitting patterns resemble those from the Nordic countries.

The material used for the cap is a rather coarse yarn in two colors – one light and one dark. The easiest way to follow the repeat is to divide the stitches on five needles, so that each repeat of 22 stitches is on its own needle.

The one-needle method is used to cast on (see page 30), and it is worked in twisted knitting, (see page 32). On the 3rd round the yarn is brought from behind, so that the twisting turns the other way.

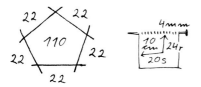

Because of the cuff, the work should be turned inside out (so that the right side becomes the wrong side) after the ladder pattern is knit.

Turn here.

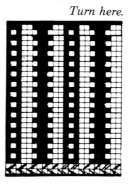

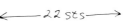

← 22 sts →

By comparing the tops of the two caps, you can see how a small detail, like the star, is made into a new pattern – the ladder – and completely changes the look of the crown. The ladder design shapes the crown and forms a band on either side of the decreases.

An alternative way to close the crown.

Cap with staggered pattern

There are infinite possibilities for varying and combining different elements of old knitting patterns. A new shape can be made by decreasing the crown, or new motif can be formed by simply staggering a pattern. The leaf runner pattern here is inspired by a band pattern from an old Finnish mitten.

The caps have twisted knit borders worked just after casting on, as described on page 32.

The material is an irregular, home-spun yarn that enlivens the pattern. The colors are black and white.

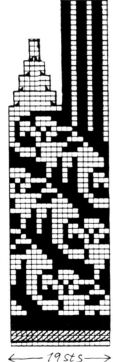

← 9 sts →

Knit 2 stitches together through back of loop immediately after the dark stripes, and 2 stitches together in the ordinary manner just before the next stripe. Knit two rounds between each decrease round.

44

← 19 sts →

Use the one-needle casting on method (see page 30) with two colors, holding the dark yarn over the thumb. 1st round: repeat 1 light, 1 dark stitch throughout the round. 2nd round: Second bring the yarn in front of the work, purl the light stitches with the light yarn and purl the dark stitches with the dark yarn. Take care to bring the yarn you are going to use in front of the other yarn so that the two yarns are twisted.

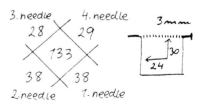

The easiest way to divide the stitches when there are 7 pattern repeats of 19 stitches each.

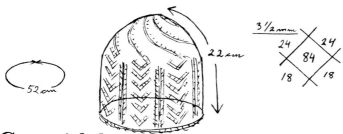

Cap with lace casting on, open-work pattern, and decreasing in spirals

Lace casting on, knit as a narrow band (see page 32), is used for this cap. This enables you to measure the head as you knit the band.

Knit the openwork pattern according to the diagram until six V shapes are completed (12 cm from the bottom edge). The vertical row of eyelet ends here, and on the following round (37th) 3 stitches are knit together after the wrapping for the eyelet, instead of the usual 2 stitches. On the following rounds of eyelet, the eyelets are moved one stitch to the left, so that the decrease holes form confluent spirals. Cast off when all the spirals are united.

The cap is knit with two strands of tightly twisted, rather thin yarn.

```
        ←         V V V
V ◣³ O V V V   V V V V    39.
V V   V V V V   V V V V    38.
V V ◣³ O V V   V V V V V   37.

V V V V V V V   V V V V V   6.
◣ O V V V O ◢   ◣ O V O ◢   5.
V V V V V V V   V V V V V   4.
V ◣ O V O ◢ V   ◣ O V O ◢   3.
V V V V V V V   V V V V V   2.
V V ◣ O V V V   ◣ O V O ◢   1.
←  7 sts  →   ←  5 sts →
←        7 ½ cm        →
```

The eyelet pattern consists of two patterns put together: one vertical row of eyelet 5 stitches wide, and a V-shaped pattern with 7 stitches. Both patterns measure six rows. For the sake of clarity, the two patterns are separated in the illustration.

Key to symbols
V = 1 knit stitch
◢ = 2 stitches together
◣ = 2 stitches together through back of loop
◣³ = slip 1 stitch on to needle, 2 stitches together, carry the slipped stitch across.

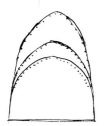

Casting off and shaping the crown

As described earlier, the easiest way to close off a cylinder – or a tube-shaped cap – is by gathering it at the top. Or, if you wish to shape the cap, you merely fold the tube flat and close the two halves at the top, giving it a pointed finish.

By dividing the shape into any number of stitches, you can make the cap fit better. This also enables you to close the top of the cap in a decorative way.

Since you normally knit in rounds, using four needles and the same number of stitches on each needle, it is natural to divide the stitches into two or three additional parts on each needle when knitting counted stitch patterns. Then the shape will be divided into eight or sixteen parts in all. Where a special effect is desired, or where the pattern should multiply beautifully with the number of stitches, these can be divided into five or six parts, as the model shows here.

A boy with a cap from Falun in Sweden. A water color painting by W. Marstrand.

Multicolored crown

The different ways to add stitches are of great aesthetic importance when you knit two or three stitches together, especially when the decreases are emphasized by change of color, as in multicolored knitting.

Three different closings will be described here, where the vertical stripes emphasize the decreases and make new striped figures.

Striped cap with slanted, asymmetrical casting off

The cuff is knit with needles .5 mm thicker than those used for the cap itself. To make the cap fit better, a 2 cm ribbing (k2, p2) is knit at the transition from fold to cap. The model is knit with rather thin, tightly twisted yarn. The stitch total is 168, but this can easily be changed, as the repeat is only 4 stitches.

Cast on 168 stitches, using 3 mm needles. Knit as the diagram shows, alternating two dark and two light stitches, until the fold is 15 cm wide. Then knit the ribbing 2 cm wide, (k2, p2) with the dark color and turn the knitting over, wrong side out. Knit with the two colors again, but this time with 2.5 mm needles, until the work measures 9.5 cm from the ribbing, and start decreasing for the crown.

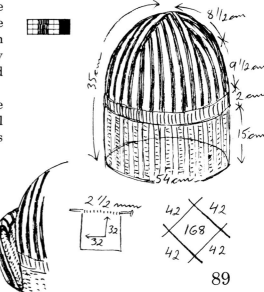

89

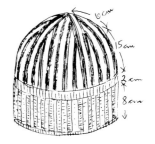

The crown

The decreases shown here are based on the same technique: knit 2 stitches together and carry the second stitch of the left needle across the first stitch; the decrease will slant toward the right. On every new round, 1 stitch less is knit before decreasing.

The cap is divided into six decrease parts, which gives each part

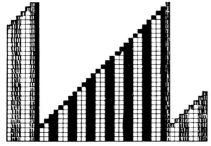

A single part of the decrease.

168 divided by 6, or 28 stitches. The two stripes of the repeat, a dark and a light, are decreased and fused with the following dark stripe:

1st round: 1 light and 1 dark stitch are knit together with the dark yarn.

2nd round: 1 light and 1 dark stitch are knit together with the dark yarn.

3d round: 2 dark stitches are knit together with the dark yarn.

4th round: knit the two dark stitches together with dark yarn.

The first four decrease rounds.

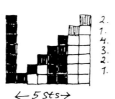

Now two stripes have disappeared, a light and a dark one, and by using the dark yarn for each decrease, the following dark stripe preserves its two dark stitches.

Repeat these four decrease rounds until there is only one stitch left in each part, a total of 6 stitches. Cast off by drawing the yarn through all the stitches. The cuff should be folded up and the inside of the fold should be seamed to the outside.

Striped cap with symmetrical casting off

This cap is knit with the same type of yarn and the same number of stitches as the previous model. In this case, however, the decreases are made from both sides until all the decreases meet at the top in straight lines.

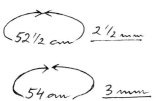

Cast on 168 stitches using 2.5 mm needles and the dark yarn, and work six rounds (k2, p2) for the top of the first fold. Purl the next round to make a sharp edge, then knit two rounds still using the dark yarn. Now with size 3 mm needles, knit 7 cm, alternating two light stitches and two dark stitches, and finish by knitting two rounds. Then purl one round for the bottom of the fold, and change back to 2.5 mm needles. Work 2 cm of ribbing (k2, p2).

Turn the work over, and continue knitting the vertical stripes until the work measures 15 cm from the end of the ribbing. Then start decreasing the crown.

The crown

The decrease method is the same as for the previous example; however, in this case, 3 stitches are knit together at once, so that one whole stripe disappears on the first round and there are no decreases on the following round.

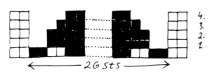

A dark and a light stripe are decreased and fused with the following dark stripe.

At the right side, the stitches are knit together through the back of the loop. At the left side, knit as ordinary knit stitch, and the stitches will slant in the right direction. You should always decrease using the dark yarn.

This crown is also divided into six parts, each with 28 stitches. The decrease repeat is 26 stitches, framed by bands two stitches wide. Inside these frames, all the dark stripes are united in points.

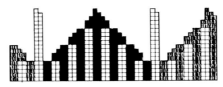

A single decrease part.

1st round: after the first 2 stitches, which form the white band, knit 3 stitches together through back of loop using the dark yarn (equals 3 dark stitches). Repeat. The last 3 stitches are knit with the dark yarn.

2nd round: knit without decreases.

3d round: knit 2 dark stitches together (equals 2 dark stitches). Repeat. Knit the last 2 stitches together using the dark yarn.

4th round: knit 2 dark stitches together, 1 dark, continue knitting and join the last two stitches with dark yarn.

Continue in this manner until there are 2 light and 2 dark stitches left in each decrease part, 24 stitches all told. On the last round, 2 dark stitches should be knit together with dark yarn and 2 light stitches should be knit together with light yarn, which leaves 12 stitches to be cast off.

To hide the first rib, you should fold it into the cuff and seam it.

Striped cap with decreasing at alternating angles

The previous models show how a vertical stripe (consisting of 2 stitches) can be continued unbroken throughout the knitting by simply decreasing. This technique will be employed here, but this time with stripes, alternating between one dark stitch and one light stitch.

The drawing will help you understand this technique. The example may look like advanced geometry, but if you have the knitting in front of you, you will understand what it is all about – and you will discover the many variations made possible by this method.

91

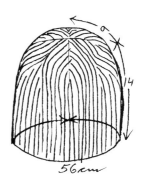

This cap does not have a cuff as have the two others, but it is knit in the same way as the cap on page 84, only in this case the crown is shaped.

The crown

Each decrease part consists of 40 stitches, that are divided again into two parts of 20 stitches each, with their own decrease technique.

The first decreases are made with the middle 20 stitches, which meet symmetrically in a pointed tip as shown on the previous model.

The light yarn should be used

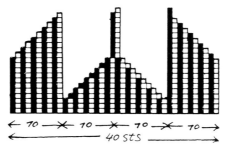

Shown here is a decrease part, where the calculations are made by dividing the stitches onto the four needles.

when the decreases slant to the left, and 1 light and 1 dark stitch are knit together.

The dark yarn is used when 1 dark and 1 light stitch are knit together slanting to the right.

On the next decrease round the decreases are made in the beginning and at the end of each needle. The following technique is also used in this case: 1 light and 1 dark stitch are knit together with the light yarn, slanted toward the right. The dark yarn is used when 1 light and 1 dark stitch are knit together, slanted toward the left.

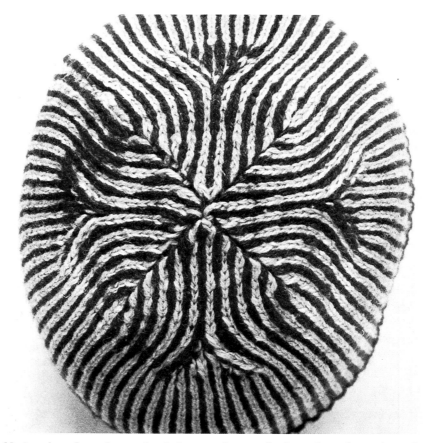

Notice that the subtracted stitches continue, unbroken, throughout the stripe repeat.

92

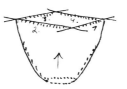

A copy of an old cap from Halland in Sweden.

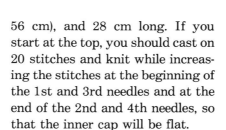

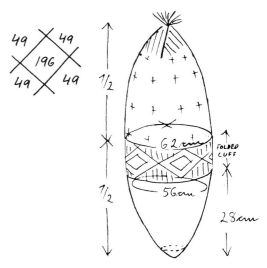

Double cap with turned up, patterned borders

This cap actually consists of two caps, one inside the other. It is made long enough to have a big folded cuff, like the one on page 83.

This knit cap is the ultimate in thickness and warmth. The cap shown here is ideal for skiing, for example, and is useful for people of all ages.

First knit the inner cap, calculating from the measurement of the head (the normal measurement is 56 cm), and 28 cm long. If you start at the top, you should cast on 20 stitches and knit while increasing the stitches at the beginning of the 1st and 3rd needles and at the end of the 2nd and 4th needles, so that the inner cap will be flat.

When you start knitting the border, change to needles that are 5 mm thicker, because the border is going to cover two more layers of knitting. It might be necessary to add extra stitches so that the circumference measures 62 cm.

Considering the materials available, there are endless pattern possibilities, depending on your choice of colors and yarn. Shown here are some simple patterned borders that can be used or changed according to your wishes. Remember, however, that when you use figured borders, like hearts, you should knit them upside down.

The decreases required for shaping the cap should be made between the borders so as not to interfere with the pattern. The decreases for the crown can be made by using the decrease techniques shown on the other caps.

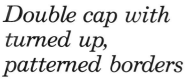

Folded cuff.

Double-knit cap using two balls of yarn

If you wish to make an exceptionally warm cap, you can knit it double – an inner cap and an outer cap – so that an insulating layer of air lies between them.

You can knit two caps that are alike, and put one into the other, or you can knit them both at the same time. This is done by having twice the number of stitches on the needle and knitting every other stitch with one yarn and the opposite stitches with another yarn. You can knit with two different colors, and leave the decision of choosing the right side color until later.

Compare this technique with that used for the one-colored mittens with the cloverleaf border on page 108. Two strands of yarn are used here, too, but in this case, they are twisted to tie the double knitting together. Here, two separate layers are knit at the same time.

The cap is knit on a circular needle 60 cm long, with two different colors of yarn, to make the inside dark and the outside light. The yarn is hand-spun and irregular, but the irregularities are balanced out by the double knitting. To get as light a cap as pos-

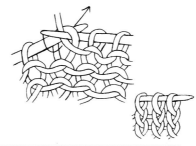

The decreases are made right after the first dark stripe.

sible, the size of needles is rather thick – 7 mm. The total number of stitches is 108 (which gives half that number for each cap, or 54 stitches).

Use the one-needle casting on method (see page 30), with the two colors, light and dark. Hold the yarn as for ordinary multicolored knitting. Carry both yarns across the left index finger – the light yarn, which forms the right side, in front of the dark yarn, which additionally is carried across the middle finger. Then knit the light yarn and purl the dark yarn, working the two pieces, inside and the outside, at the same time, but separately.

Work 20 cm in this way, then

When the wrong side purl stitch is purled, the yarn for the right side should be carried forward.

To make the work easier and to get the shortest possible movements, the yarn is carried under the right needle when the stitch is purled. The stitches will lie as crossed knit stitches on the right side of the work.

decrease on every third round (change to stocking needles of the same size). On the first decrease round, the decreases are made after every eighth stitch by purling 1 light and 1 dark stitch together and knitting the following two stitches together. On the second decrease round, the decreases are made after every seventh stitch in the same way, and on the third decrease round, after every sixth stitch. The remaining stitches are cast off the usual way, by breaking the yarn and drawing it through the open stitches.

A variation of double knitting with two balls of yarn

If you find it uncomfortable to knit with two balls of yarn at the same time, you can knit the outer cap on the first round using light yarn and the dark inner cap on the following round.

1st round: use a light yarn. k1, slip the next stitch purl-wise onto the needle, carrying the yarn forward. Repeat to the end of the round.

2nd round: use a dark yarn. Slip the light knit stitch onto the needle, carrying the yarn behind the work, and purl the following stitch. Repeat to the end of the round.

Alternate these two rounds the whole time.

This method is more time-consuming, but for most people it is easier to knit this way.

Double-knit cap using two needles

Hand-spun, woollen yarn is used for this cap also. It is knit back and forth with only one ball of yarn, and the right and wrong sides are alike. Different colors of wool are spun together to give this yarn its character.

Cast on 108 stitches with size 7 mm needles, and knit back and forth.

1st row: k1, slip 1 stitch purlwise onto the needle, yarn forward. Repeat to the end of the row.

Work all the following rows in this manner, so that every other stitch is knit on every other row. When the work measures 20 cm, the stitches are decreased at regular intervals on two rows. 1st decrease row: k8, slip 1 stitch purlwise onto the needle, place the following stitch, temporarily unknit, on the right needle. Place the stitch, which is going to be slipped, onto a stitch holder, and knit the stitch from the right needle together with the next knit stitch. Carry the "loose" stitch back on the left needle and slip two stitches onto the right needle at the same time. Repeat to the end of the row. 2nd decrease row: The double loose stitches are knit together, to restore the succession of the stitches.

Each decrease part can be emphasized by working a double row of knit stitches in a different color. All the stitches should be knit using this color, and the turned rows should be made with the main color on all the other rows.

Knit six rows without decreasing, then on the following decrease rounds, 1 stitch less is knit between each decrease.

When the cap is the desired length, the stitches should be cast off and the sides seamed as invisibly as possible.

Caps knit vertically

Just like the blouses on page 71, caps can be knit as tubes in vertical rows.

Here are some details to be considered when you make your calculations.

Cast on by making loops, as shown, and knit according to the diagram.

When the crown is shaped, one

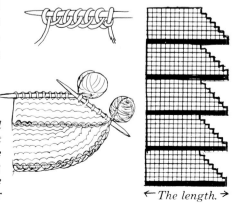

← The length. →

less stitch is knit than in the preceding row. The following stitch should always be slipped when you turn the work in the middle of a row, and the yarn should be carried forward. Now place the loose stitch back onto the left needle, turn the work over, and knit back.

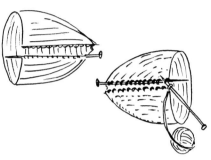

Gathering and casting off the knitting. Turn the work inside out, so that the cast-on edge is in front. Insert the needle through the first loop of the cast-on edge and on through the first stitch on the needle. Knit one stitch. Knit all the stitches like this, and cast them off at the same point as usual by carrying the first stitch across the second stitch.

The basic shape can be elongated or edged in a number of ways.

Mittens

Mittens can be fun to knit, as a mitten is a relatively moderate piece of work, and not difficult once you have become familiar with the basic techniques of shaping it. The shape of the thumb and its position relative to the top of the mitten are of great importance in achieving a good fit.

Woollen mittens are unsurpassed for serviceability. You can achieve the qualities that meet your own special needs through your handling of the wool, either in a strictly technical sense, by knitting looser or tighter, or by treating the newly-made mittens in a certain manner. Last, but not least, it is a pleasure to select your own colors and patterns!

   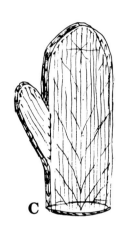 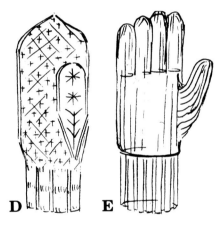

A   B   C   D   E

A. Here is the simplest mitten shape, with the thumb knit directly onto the basic tubular form. This mitten should be knit in a reasonably large size, because its width remains constant. However, you should also consider the elasticity of the knitting.

This mitten is easy to take off and put on. Multicolored knitting is suitable for this shape, because patterns are easy to work into the simple basic model.

B. Mittens fit better and are warmer if they are gathered around the wrist by a ribbed border. The thumb is made more flexible by the addition of a gusset-shaped increase.

If the decreases at the top are distributed evenly, there will be no difference between the right and left hands.

C. You can place the thumb gusset at the outer edge of the mitten and you can place the decreases to shape the mitten like the silhouette of the hand. You can make a few stitches between the palm and the back, for the width of the hand. There is no difference between the right and left hands in this case either, and a pattern design will be relatively independent of the decreases.

D. Here, the thumb gusset has been moved to the palm of the hand to make the mitten fit better, and a ribbed border is added. This model is well known as the "typical" Norwegian mitten.

E. Gloves naturally require more calculations and more precise shaping, but it can be enjoyable to work out a really good individual fit – and it is worth it!

Needles, yarn, and measuring proportions

Normally you make mittens and gloves by knitting in rounds, with all the stitches divided onto four needles and knitting with a fifth needle. To help prevent the fingers from wearing out, gloves can be knit more firmly with needles a size smaller. Also, the ribbing at the wrist is often knit with needles that are one or two sizes smaller.

Most of the models in the book for which needle size and yarn type are given are calculated to fit the average woman's hand. The models can, however, be used for a child's hand or a large male hand if a few changes are made and with adjustments in yarn and needle sizes.

A women's mitten model knit with two-ply yarn can, for example, be used for a man's mitten by simply using a three-ply yarn and thicker needles.

When you choose yarn, remember that yarn that is spun too loosely mats easily and gets hard when worn (on the other hand, lightly-matted knitting insulates better). Use a good quality yarn and always knit the mittens in a reasonably large size. It is also a good idea to use needles that are thicker than the ones you would normally use, so that your knitting is not too tight.

Decreasing at the top of the mitten

As mentioned earlier, the difference between the right and left mitten results from the shaping of the thumb, and its placement in relation to the closing at the top of the mitten. There are two different ways of decreasing: a *round decrease* is made by distributing the decreases evenly according to the same technique as used for casting off a cap's crown (see page 85). The other method, *flat decreasing*, is done by decreasing at the sides, perhaps with a few stitches between them to form a pattern band and emphasize the width of the mitten.

Round decreasing

Make sure that the total number of stitches can be divided by four; that is, all four needles should have the same number of stitches. Then knit two stitches together in the middle and at the end of each needle throughout the round. Count the number of stitches between the decreases, and then knit that number of rounds without decreasing. The next decrease

For those who wish to calculate their own measurements, it is a good idea to sketch out a basic diagram. The proportions of the hand are rather fixed, just like the other measurements of the human body, and you will see this if you compare the proportions of your own hand with this mitten diagram.

round is worked the same way as before, and for every new decrease round one round less should be knit between the decreases. Continue until there are only 2 stitches left on each needle; 8 stitches all told. Break the yarn, draw it through all the stitches, and fasten the yarn end.

Flat decrease

When you knit mittens with patterns, you may need to make the decreases at the side edges in order to avoid interfering with the pattern at the top. The front and back sides are knit alike and the stitches are divided so that the 1st and 2nd needles have the same number of stitches as the 3rd and 4th needles.

For instance:
1st needle: k2, 2 stitches together through back of loop, and knit the remaining stitches.
2nd needle: knit all stitches until there are 4 stitches left, k2 together, k2.
3d and 4th needles are worked like the two first needles.

The two stitches before and after the decreases are united, so that four stitches on either side form a band. Here a pattern can be made that is independent of the palm and back of the mitten, and the number of stitches in the band can naturally be varied.

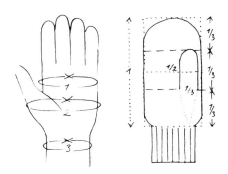

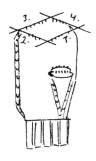

Different thumbs

Thumbs without gussets

The simplest thumb has no gusset. After the ribbing, knit the mitten in rounds, without increases, until you reach the place where the thumb should begin.

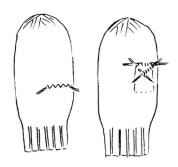

Waste yarn used in the thumb gusset.

Using waste yarn, knit the number of stitches you have calculated for the width of the thumb. Put the stitches back onto the left needle and knit them with the mitten yarn. When the mitten is finished, remove the waste yarn and divide the open stitches onto three or four needles. Pick up a few stitches from the sides, to avoid having gaps and to make the thumb wider. Work these stitches through the back of the loop to tighten them. It is advisable, also, to pick up several stitches to make the thumb nice and wide at the bottom. (Knit these stitches together on the fol-

lowing rounds). Knit the thumb as long as is required. Start decreasing halfway up the thumbnail; you can try on the mitten to measure this. The decreases are made by knitting the last 2 stitches together on every needle. Cast off the stitches like you cast off the top of the mitten.

Thumb gusset

If you have calculated the mitten to be tight around the wrist, stitches should be added at the widest part of the hand, where the thumb starts.

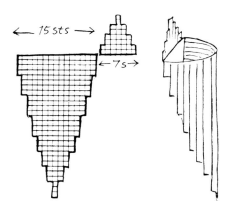

Gusset with increases on both sides of a single stitch.

The diagram shows a schematic outline of a gusset where 1 stitch is added on both sides of a single stitch. Then the increases are continued on either side of these 3

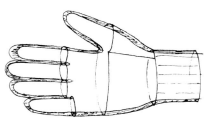

stitches and so on. The increases should be worked in the same vertical row of stitches, so that 2 more stitches are made between the increases every time, depending on how long the gusset is required to be. When the gusset is long enough, place the stitches on a safety pin or a thick thread, and continue knitting.

When you are ready to knit the thumb, cast on new stitches above the gusset. Now is the time to ad-

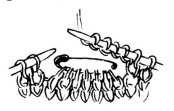

Cast on new stitches above the thumb gusset: the gusset stitches are placed on a safety pin.

just the number of stitches for the thumb. If you wish to make the thumb wide at the base, you can cast on plenty of stitches and decrease them on the following rounds. In this manner, you can make a small gusset, like the large gusset, only this time by decreasing.

You can increase by knitting 2 stitches through the same stitch (through front and back of the loop). This way a small "pip" will appear, which can be helpful when you knit with only one color and

98

have to keep track of the vertical increase row.

You can also pick up the strand of yarn between two stitches, turned, and knit this extra stitch. In multicolored knitting this method is especially good, because you can pick up the color of yarn you are going to use on the following vertical rows without tightening the other stitches.

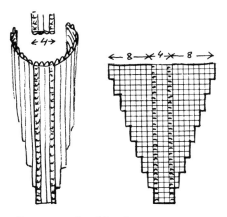

Gusset at the side edge.

You can place the thumb gusset at the side edge of the mitten, so that it is independent of the rest of the stitches. In this case, you should place the decreases on both sides of four basic stitches. These stitches continue up along the sides of the mitten until they are decreased as described in the flat decrease method.

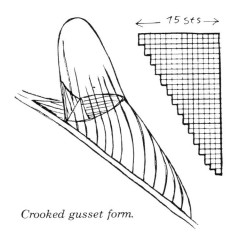

Crooked gusset form.

Above is shown a crooked gusset shape, where all increases are made in the same vertical row of stitches, but on one side only. To make the length of the gusset the same all the way, the increases should be made on every other round.

If the increases are made toward the palm of the hand, the thumb will be more flexible and the rows of stitches will be unbroken on the back of the mitten. See the example on the gloves on page 110.

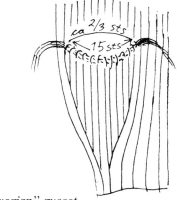

"Norwegian" gusset.

Here is a gusset shape that is used especially in the "Norwegian" type of mitten. Large pattern designs are knit on the back of the

mitten, and small patterns are adjusted to fit into the gusset-shaped increases in the palm of the hand.

The flat decrease method is used for this type of placement of the pattern shapes, and there is a distinct difference between a right and a left mitten. Here a gusset is made starting at the end of the second needle for the left mitten, and at the beginning of the first needle for the right mitten.

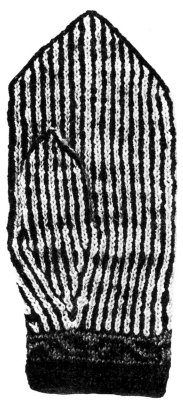

On this mitten the shapes are divided by stripes.

99

Three simple mittens of loosely spun yarn

In different parts of the Nordic countries, but perhaps in Iceland especially, garments made of loosely spun, soft yarn were brushed up. This makes the fabric more durable, firmer, and warmer.

Mittens treated in this way should be knit with thick yarn and in simple shapes without thumb gussets; they should be rather large and without any special shaping.

All the mittens are knit with the same number of stitches (36) until they are shaped at the top. The large cuff on the checkered mitten is worked with needles that are one-half size thicker than those used for the mitten itself. Multicolored knitting contracts more than plain knitting, and this emphasizes the difference in width even more.

To make the thumb fit better, and prevent it from wearing out, it can be knit with needles that are one-half size thinner than those used for the rest of the mitten. The two mittens that are plain at the top are made with round decreases, but the best way to shape the multicolored mitten is to decrease at the sides, to avoid interfering with the pattern. Here the flat decrease method should be used.

A folded cuff with a decorative effect

You can knit many decorative details on the cuff of a mitten, as you can on the folded cuff of a cap.

The mitten is embroidered, using a simple sewing technique where the decorative yarn is pulled through vertical basting stitches, as shown on the diagram.

To prevent the fold from ripping, you should cast on with triple yarn and make a loop border.

1st round: p1, slip 1 stitch onto the needle, yarn forward. Repeat to the end of the round.

2nd round: slip 1 stitch onto the needle, yarn forward, p1, alternating as before.

When you change from the border to the mitten, shift the knit stitches from one side, to knit stitches on the other side, by simply turning the knitting over and working the other way.

The finished mitten is brushed up except for the embroidered cuff.

If you want to keep the knitted structure on the right side of the mitten, you should merely brush up the inside.

Treatment of the finished mittens

The woollen material is just as important as the shaping of the mitten. If you want the mittens to be particularly thick, warm, and hard wearing, choose a quality of wool that can stand being brushed up vigorously after it is knit. This makes the woolly hair stand out and form an extra insulating layer.

For further treatment, you can scrub the mittens with soap in alternating warm and cold water as described on page 125 under "fulling". You must remember, however, that the larger the garment,

the looser the knitting, and the more you full it, the more it will shrink.

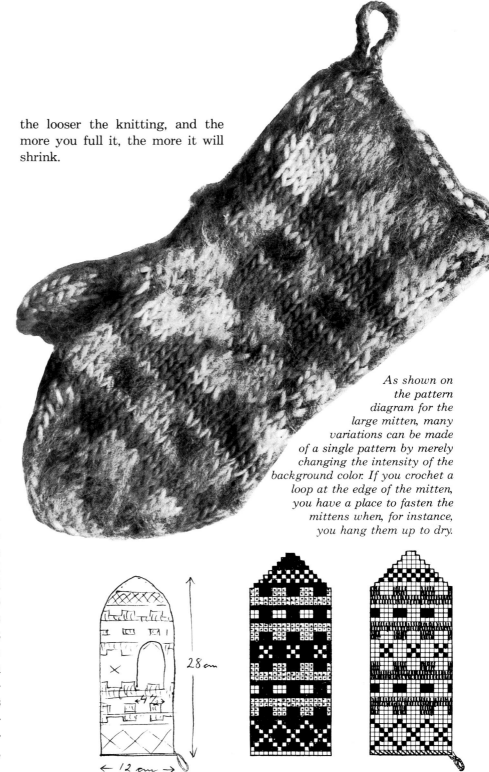

As shown on the pattern diagram for the large mitten, many variations can be made of a single pattern by merely changing the intensity of the background color. If you crochet a loop at the edge of the mitten, you have a place to fasten the mittens when, for instance, you hang them up to dry.

101

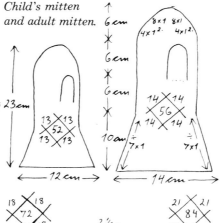

Child's mitten and adult mitten.

Embroidered mittens with fringed cuffs

Hand-knit mittens are – and always have been – a popular gift. They are both a practical article for everyday use and an expression of creativity. It is told in old narratives that farmers often used mittens as wedding presents.

In Norway and in Dalarna in Sweden, very tight and finely knit mittens were often embroidered.

The models shown here have shapes copied from Norwegian mittens from Valdres, where this type of mitten was a great tourist article. The mittens are embroidered mainly with satin stitch, which makes it possible to form shapes of solid color. According to the old tradition, flowers are common motifs for embroidery, and the shapes can be varied endlessly.

To achieve a good and tight background material, the mittens should be knit rather firmly. The thumb should be placed in the palm of the hand so as not to ruin the decoration on the back of the mitten. A gusset can be knit to make the thumb fit better, but it is really not necessary, because of the generous size. The decreases at the top are best made at the sides. The first four decreases should be made on either side on every other round, and the following decreases on every round, until there are 8 stitches left. These stitches should be cast off at one time.

In early days, a fringed edge was commonly used to complete knit mittens and caps, and this can be made in various ways.

A carved cupboard door from the Gudbrands Valley in Norway.

The gloves are a beautiful example of the wealth of design found in old Norwegian folk art. The same intricate leaf designs that are seen in wood carvings and on painted furniture are rendered in the gloves by means of solid covering of satin stitch on the back of the hand and on the thumb.

102

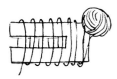

By making a cardboard template with a slit, and winding yarn around it, you can make a fringe. Wind the yarn (not too tightly or too thick) around the cardboard and machine-stitch a seam down the slit to fasten the yarn. Then carefully pull the cardboard away from the sewn part and wind more yarn around it, and so on, until you have made a long sewed fringe.

Sew the fringe onto the edge of the mitten. Use close, firm stitches worked through the center seam of the fringe. Finally, cut the fringe down the sides, so that the short yarn ends "plush" and cover the seam.

A closed fringe, or looped fringe, is made here, using two threads at once and worked from the wrong side of the knitting: Knit 2 stitches, one through the front of the loop, the other through the back of the loop, carrying the yarn from below your index finger. Slip both stitches onto the right needle at the same time and knit them together. Knit the rows on the right side of the work in the usual way. Here, three rows of loops are made.

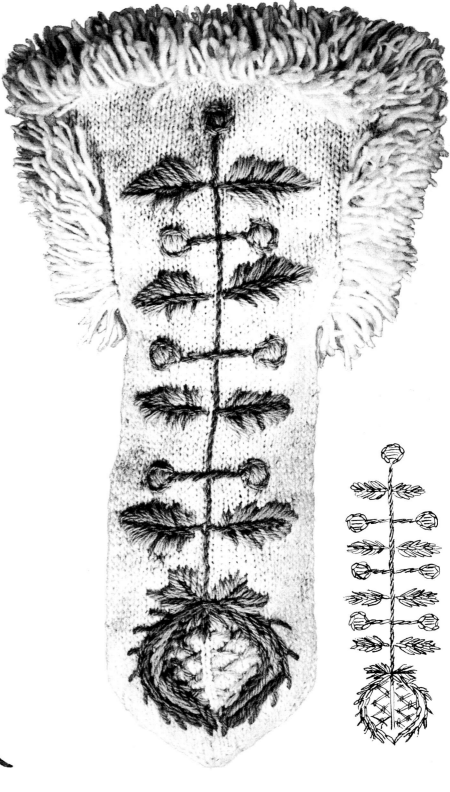

103

Fully patterned mittens

The play with optical effects, which began when the Italian Renaissance painters discovered and used perspective in their work, was adopted in the common arts all over Europe. Here are shown different examples of such pattern forms.

Interior from the Nyborg Castle.

A man's mitten from Estonia shows the same pattern idea.

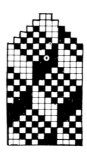

← *10.5 cm* →

3 mm

14 ✕ 14
56
14 ✕ 14

It is not difficult to adjust a model to your own measurement, by changing yarn – and needle size – or by working more or fewer pattern repeats across. Usually the result will be best if you make the decreases at the side edges like flat decreases.

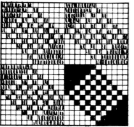

Pattern from Gotland.

Pattern from Norway.

Notice how the slanted shapes are technically suited to multicolored knitting.

The model mitten has an inside fold and a narrow edge pattern.

The old star pattern, which is repeated in many variations, is used here in a fully patterned mitten.

A similar pattern repeat is seen on the mitten from Lolland, with the Bethlehem star and the "stake" or the "ladder", which is also used in the cap on page 86. The ladder pattern is elongated toward the top of the side edges, where the decreases are made.

After casting on, two rounds of twisted knitting are worked.

1st round: carry the working yarn in front of the other yarn.
2nd round: carry the working yarn behind the other yarn. See also page 32.

A mitten from Lolland with star and ladder pattern. It is rare to find information about the origin of as simple an everyday garment as a pair of mittens. And it is far from certain that the patterns had symbolic meanings.

Many of the old knit garments were made with very thin yarn and thin needles.

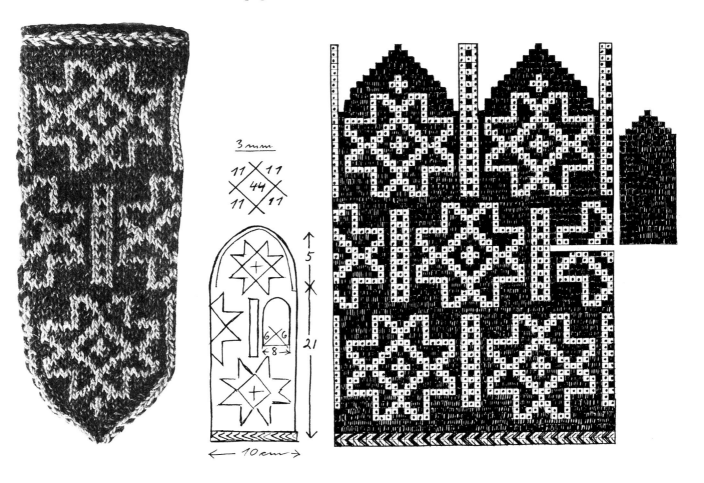

Mittens with bird pattern

This mitten is perhaps one of the best-known and characteristic Norwegian and Swedish mitten forms. The mitten has a complicated pattern on the back; the palm, the thumb with its gusset, and the side bands each have their own little motif. The knitting is facilitated by working each shaping part separately, each with its own pattern, and many variations can be made.

Here, about 50 grams of two-ply yarn is used of each color, light and dark, and 5 needles, size 3 mm.

The left mitten should be knit as follows. Cast on 52 stitches, using 4 needles, and work 20 rounds of ribbing, k2, p2 as shown on the mitten diagram, and end by knitting 2 rounds with the dark yarn.

On the following round, knit, while adding 4 stitches spread out evenly over the round. Begin the multicolored pattern: on the first needle, the first 16 stitches should be knit as shown on the diagram, starting at the little x to the right. On the second needle, the 3 stitches marked A on the diagram should be knit (the same 3 stitches marked A show the thumb gusset

A pair of Swedish mittens with a new pattern for each part of the mitten.

pattern on the thumb diagram), and the 2 stitches that finish out the palm of the hand, plus the 3 side band stitches, are knit. The 29 stitches, plus 2 side band stitches of the back of the mitten, should be placed on the other half of the mitten, on the 3rd and 4th needles.

The gusset is drawn in the thumb diagram. On the first increase round knit 1 light stitch and 1 dark stitch through the 1st light stitch, knit the next stitch light, then knit 1 dark stitch and 1 light

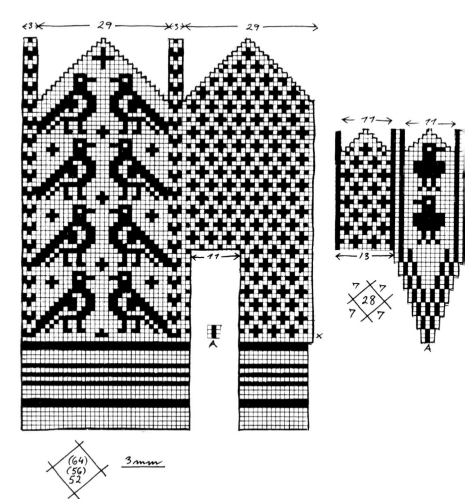

stitch through the last of the 3 "A" stitches. See page 98 about increases. Repeat these increases on every 4th round (follow the diagram) until gusset has 13 stitches.

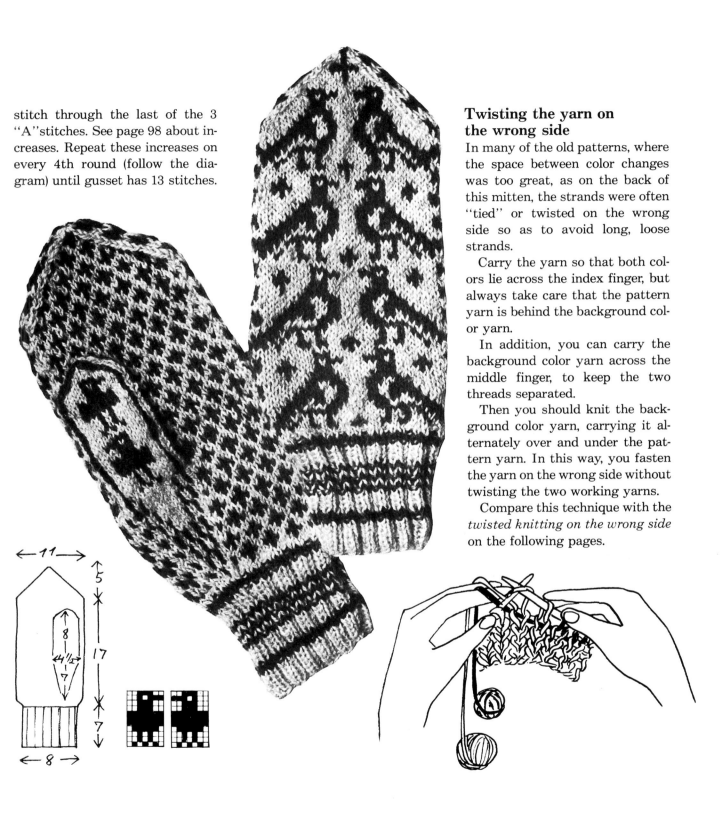

Twisting the yarn on the wrong side

In many of the old patterns, where the space between color changes was too great, as on the back of this mitten, the strands were often "tied" or twisted on the wrong side so as to avoid long, loose strands.

Carry the yarn so that both colors lie across the index finger, but always take care that the pattern yarn is behind the background color yarn.

In addition, you can carry the background color yarn across the middle finger, to keep the two threads separated.

Then you should knit the background color yarn, carrying it alternately over and under the pattern yarn. In this way, you fasten the yarn on the wrong side without twisting the two working yarns.

Compare this technique with the *twisted knitting on the wrong side* on the following pages.

Mittens with cloverleaf border – different ways to knit with two strands of yarn

In addition to the aesthetic value, multicolored knitting has, as mentioned before, the practical advantage of making a double material that is warm and durable.

The plain part of this mitten is made by using two strands of yarn of the same color and by changing yarns with every other stitch, to preserve the same thickness as is on the border.

You can use two different techniques: ordinary multicolored knitting or twisted knitting.

 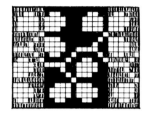

The cloverleaf border comes from an old knitting sample roll from the Nordenfjeld Museum of Decorative Arts in Trondhiem. The same pattern is found in mittens from Estonia! Where is the cultural connection? How do and did these old knitting patterns, especially in early days, travel? It is often by coincidence that a pattern is referred to as typical for a region or a country!

Twisting as a knitting technique

Knitting that is twisted on the wrong side of the work is made by tying the two strands of yarn on the wrong side, as described on the previous page, and at the same time by regularly carrying the working yarn *under* the other yarn with every other stitch. The technique used for this type of twisted knitting is basically the same as for the twisted borders described on page 32, where the twisting is done on the right side as a decorative border.

Ordinary multicolored knitting and twisted knitting will appear as ordinary stockinette stitch on the right side.

Here is shown a piece of ordinary multicolored knitting, where the strands on the wrong side run horizontally.

Twisted knitting is more time-consuming, because the working yarn also twists. The balls of yarn should be separated and untangled regularly. But the knitting will appear smoother on the right side and be more elastic than with the ordinary multicolored knitting method.

The sample is knit with two strands of yarn in different colors to make the technique clear.

Both in Norway and Sweden, where socks and mittens had to be especially warm and durable, this old technique was used.

Norwegian mitten with twisted knitting on the right side.

Above is a sample using the combination of a decoratively twisted knit border and plain twisted knitting on the wrong side.

After casting on, with double yarn, two rounds of twisted knitting should be worked using 1 strand of light yarn and 1 of dark.

The yarn will untangle automatically if you twist the stitches in one direction on the first round and the other direction on the second round. After knitting one round with the light yarn, two rounds of twisted knitting should be worked using the light yarn, followed by one round, alternating k1 light stitch, k1 dark stitch. The next round of twisted knitting should be worked by purling the light stitch of the previous round using dark yarn, and purling dark stitches with light yarn. The last round should be worked twisted, using the dark yarn, and the rest of the work should be twisted knitting, using the light yarn on the wrong side.

Gloves in a single color with ribbed cuffs

Many people are afraid to try knitting gloves, because it seems difficult to divide up the stitches for the fingers to get the correct fit, which is more important in this case than for mittens. But once you have looked at the basic diagram and become familiar with the main rules, gloves should not be difficult and will be worth the effort.

Normally you should use a number of stitches that can be divided by four, for instance 48, 56, or 64, depending on the size of the gloves and the yarn you have chosen.

The model is knit with thin, soft yarn and size 2 mm needles, and it should fit the average female hand. 48 stitches should be cast on.

The left glove

Knit a ribbed border, k2, p2, 24 or 36 rounds, depending on the width you want the ribbing. Finish the ribbing by purling one round.

Start increasing for the thumb gusset at the end of the second needle, and 3 or 4 rounds after the ribbed border. As described on page 99 in the section about gussets, the increases should be made on one side, all of them turning toward the palm of the glove in vertical stitch rows, on every other round. Purl the second to last stitch on the second needle, knit the strand of yarn between the two last stitches twisted, and knit the last stitch. Work the next round without increases, but purl the purl stitch from the previous round (by doing this you mark the increases and can follow them easily). Repeat these two rounds until you have knit 24 rounds, and have added 12 stitches.

Make the hole for the thumb by putting the 12 stitches, the purled stitch, and the last stitch of second needle (total 14 stitches) on a thick thread or a safety pin. Cast on 11 new stitches, place the 11th stitch on the 3rd needle and knit

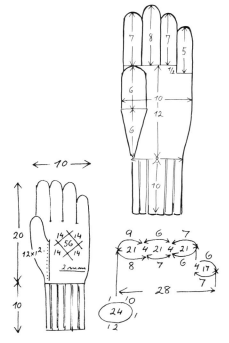

this stitch together with the first stitch. Continue knitting until you reach the beginning of the little finger (about 48 rounds from the ribbed border).

Form a little gusset by decreasing stitches above the hole for the thumb until there are 56 stitches all told.

It is important that the stitches are divided evenly onto the needles, and that the outer end stitch of the thumb hole always remains as the last stitch on the second needle (or the last stitch of the palm of the hand). This way the rest of the fingers will be correctly placed in relation to the thumb. The mitten will fit better if you start knitting the little finger about one-half cm before the rest of the fingers.

For the little finger, use the last 6 stitches of the fourth needle and the first 7 stitches of the first needle, and cast on 4 new stitches. Divide these stitches onto three needles and work about 5 cm before you decrease for the tip.

First round: 2 stitches together, k2. 2nd round: 2 stitches together, k2. The last round: knit all the stitches together 2 and 2, until there are 6 or 8 stitches left. Break the yarn, draw it through the stitches and fasten the yarn end.

When the little finger is finished, four loops should be picked up from the newly cast-on stitches and a couple of rounds should be knit before you start the other fingers. Put the stitches you are not

going to use on a thick thread, and tie it where the next finger starts. Work each finger like the little finger – the distribution of the stitches for the different fingers and the new stitches for each finger can be seen on the diagram. The length of the fingers varies from 6 to 7 cm. Measure on your own hand: the decreases should start halfway up the nail. If there are too many stitches when you have picked up for the thumb, you can knit a small gusset at the inner side of the thumb. The length of a thumb is usually the same as the length from the base of the hand to the thumb's hole (or the length of the gusset).

The gusset and all the fingers will be reversed when you knit the right glove.

The easiest way to distribute the stitches for the different fingers is to put on the mitten and insert knitting needles between the fingers, count the stitches, and write down the numbers on the diagram.

Between every two fingers you should count on adding from 2 to 4 new stitches, depending on the yarn you are going to use.

The gloves are made without a thumb gusset, and with 2 dark and 2 light stitches alternated in vertical stripes, that stop at the finger division. The palm and the back of the glove are knit thicker, to make them warmer and more durable. A narrow stripe in a different color can be embroidered on the completed glove for decoration and finishing of the stripes.

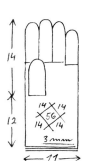

Distribution of the stitches for the fingers of the striped glove.

Gloves with the "Selbu Star"

The star is perhaps the most common motif for multicolored gloves, and it can be drawn easily on graph paper. The pattern is knit in many variations, especially for Norwegian gloves.

On the little measurement diagram you can see how this motif is suited to the proportions of the back of the glove.

For this pair of gloves, about 50 grams of three-ply yarn of each color, light and dark, is used, and the 5 needles are size 3 mm.

Cast on 50 stitches using the light yarn and knit the first 2 rounds as the narrow loop edge described on page 36. Knit according to the diagram on the previous page. When you have finished the star on the back of the glove, divide the stitches for the fingers, as shown on the diagram. Knit the fingers according to the index finger diagram; however, you should reduce, slightly, the number of stitches for the little finger.

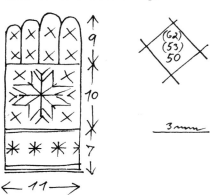

112

A small selection of typical Norwegian mitten motifs with different numbers of stitches. According to your own taste and the yarn you have chosen, you can combine different pattern parts without much difficulty by framing – or unframing – the patterns, or by increasing the number of stitches in the side bands.

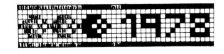

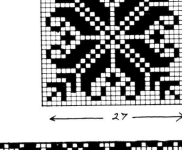

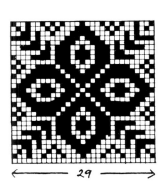

 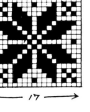

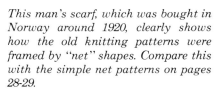

This man's scarf, which was bought in Norway around 1920, clearly shows how the old knitting patterns were framed by "net" shapes. Compare this with the simple net patterns on pages 28-29.

Stockings

"*A woollen sock absorbs twice as much perspiration as a cotton sock which is just as thick, which in turn absorbs twice as much as the best socks made of synthetic materials*".
The Danish National Council for Domestic Science, 1978.

Stocking knitting has been out of favor for many years. Old people, who remember stockings that scratched the child's delicate skin, and housewives, who think back with horror to the everlasting mending of stockings during the wars, praise the cheap machine-made nylon stockings – and the art of stocking knitting slowly wastes away...

There is one problem, however, with machine-made stockings. In order to keep the price down, the quality must suffer. Such stockings are of less generous size and do not allow free movement of the toes, or are made of synthetic materials which prevent the feet from perspiring naturally.

Leo Tolstoy
War and Peace

..." 'Anna Makarovna has finished her stocking,' said Countess Marya. 'Oh, I'm going to have a look at them,' said Pierre... Pierre went into the children ... 'Now, Anna Makarovna,' cried Pierre's voice ... 'when I say three you stand here ... Now, one, two ... three!' 'Two, two!' cried the children.

They meant the two stockings, which, by a secret known only to her, Anna Makarovna used to knit on her needles at once. She always made a solemn ceremony of pulling one stocking out of the other in the presence of the children when the pair was finished."

The maid's pattern is still a secret. How Anna separates the two stockings is still uncertain. The quotation makes one wonder how many knitting details and fine points have been lost during the years.

Woman from Funen. About 1920.

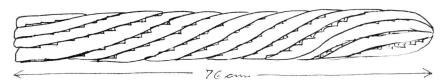

$\longleftarrow \qquad 76\ mm \qquad \longrightarrow$

Spiral knit stockings without heels

Many beginners find it difficult to shape a heel, and for those who do not wish to start, the following simple models for thick knee stockings may be a good introduction to stocking knitting!

Ribbed knitting is suitable for stockings because of the elastic quality, and is commonly used for the top of socks and stockings.

When the rib is moved one stitch to the side at regular intervals, the knitting will become spiral-shaped and the stocking will fit even better. You need only calculate the width and the length of the stocking, because heels are completely unnecessary in stockings worked in spiral rib. The stockings will fit all sizes of feet, and they will not wear in the same place all the time.

This model will make a nice night sock if it is knit quite short.

Large, long stocking

About 300 grams of thick natural yarn and 4 stocking needles, size 6 mm, are used.

Cast 48 stitches on 3 needles and k3, p3. Stagger the pattern by 1 stitch on every 5th round. After you have staggered 26 times (68 cm) decrease for the toe

1st round: k2 together, k1, p3. Repeat. Work 5 rounds without decreasing.

7th round: k2, p2 together, p1. Repeat. Work 4 rounds without decreasing.

12th round: k2 together, p2. Repeat. 3 rounds without decreasing.

16th round: k1, p2 together. Repeat. 2 rounds without decreasing.

19th round: 2 stitches together throughout the round. Break the yarn and pull it through the remaining stitches, and fasten the yarn.

Child's size

For small children this stocking is ideal, because the child can put it on by him/herself without difficulty of positioning the heel correctly. For children's stockings you can use thinner yarn and knit a narrow spiral, staggered more frequently.

16 / 16
48
16

6 mm

14 / 14
40
12

3½ mm

Calculating stocking measurements

For the novice knitter who is going to knit a pair of socks or stockings it can be difficult to make the correct measurements, calculate the number of stitches, make the necessary increases and decreases and – not least – shape the heel.

In early days it was most common to use what was handy to measure the size and length.

In an old narrative from Falster it is told that the making of a stocking in the early days usually started with a ribbed border, k2, p2. This ribbing measured the length of an index finger (about 7 cm). A man's stocking should be two knuckle measurements from the heel to the decrease of the toe, and the toe itself should be half the knuckle measurement. (One knuckle measurement is from the tip of the middle finger to the knuckle).

Even though these measurements should not be taken too literally, it is a good idea to make your own rules of thumb.

A school model
The long stocking photographed on the next page is knit according to an old "school pattern" and the different parts of the leg are marked out with stripes and color changes.

In this case a special and more precise measuring system has been used, where the proportion between the different shapes of an average leg are said to be the same, whether the calculations are made to fit a child or an adult. Once you know the number of stitches to cast on, the remaining calculations for the length of the stocking are made by simply dividing that number.

With 80 stitches cast on, divided onto four needles each with 20 stitches, you knit as follows.

I.   Knit a ribbed border with the same number of rounds as the number of stitches on three needles (60 rounds).

II. Work the rest of the stocking in stockinette stitch; the part up to the knee should be as many rounds as the number of stitches on two needles (40 rounds).

III. Decrease stitches at regular intervals from the knee to the calf over as many rounds as the number of stitches on two needles (40 rounds).

IV. The width of the calf should be adjusted over as many rounds as the number of stitches on three needles (60 rounds). Decrease the same number of stitches as are on one needle, less two.

V.   When the decreases for the calf are finished, knit the ankle, over as many rounds as there are stitches on one and one-half needles (30 rounds).

VI. When the heel is shaped, knit the foot until the toe decrease over as many rounds as the number of stitches on three needles (60 rounds).

VII. Make the decreases for the toe over 20 rounds.

A long stocking with the different parts of the leg emphasized by stripes and color changes.

116

Knee stockings, basic pattern

If you cast on 72 stitches, using a two-ply stocking yarn, this pattern size will fit an average woman. Using thin needles and thin yarn, however, you can make a child's size with the same number of stitches; with thick yarn and thick needles you can make a size to fit a man.

Ribbed border

Usually a border is knit to make the stocking fit better. The number of stitches should be divisible by four, because this border is worked k2, p2. Cast on 72 stitches, knit 1 round, and distribute the stitches evenly on the four needles. Knit the ribbing as long as desired – here it is 18 rounds wide, or equal to the number of stitches on one needle.

Calf

When the ribbing is complete, work in stockinette stitch until you start decreasing for the calf. This part is usually as many rounds wide as the number of stitches on two needles (36 rounds).

Leg

Make the decreases over as many rounds as the number of stitches on three needles (54). Decrease the same number of stitches as are on one needle minus 2 stitches (16 stitches).

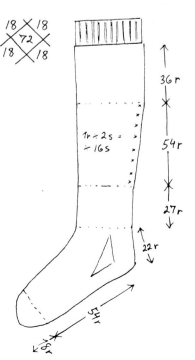

117

Decrease 2 stitches on each decrease round, which makes 8 decrease rounds to be distributed over 54 rounds. First subtract the 8 rounds from the total 54 rounds (46 rounds). These 46 rounds should be divided by the number of spaces, which is 7. This means that you should work 7 rounds without subtracting stitches between the decrease rounds, and only 4 rounds between the last two decrease rounds. On every decrease round two stitches should be knit together after the first stitch on the first needle, and the last two stitches should be knit together before the last stitch on the fourth needle.

Ankle

After the calf is knit, distribute the remaining stitches (72 minus 18, or 54) evenly on the four needles, which leaves the first and fourth needles each with 14 stitches, and the second and third needles each with 13. Remember to start and end each new row at the same place. The ankle should be as many rounds as the original number of stitches on one and one-half needles (27). Then knit the heel.

Heel

Heels can be made in several different ways, but only one method is described here and it makes a beautifully rounded heel.

The heel is always knit with the first and fourth needles; resting the other two. Knit the *heel flap* first. Work as many rows as the number of stitches on one needle plus 4 (22 rows). The first stitch on every row should always be slipped onto the needle, to make 11 side loops on each side edge. Use these for picking up stitches later on for the *side gussets*. Finish the last row as usual after the fourth needle, which is the middle of the heel flap, as shown on the diagram.

Quiet hours in the kitchen. The Faroe Islands around 1900.

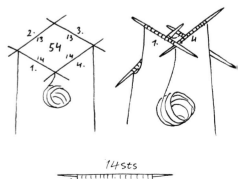

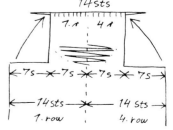

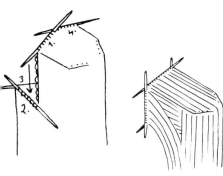

The decreases for the heel

Make the decreases at the bottom of the heel. Round the heel by working in turned rows for the first few rows, and knit 1 stitch together with the outer stitch one by one on the last rows.

Start with the first needle, knit 4 stitches, turn over. Slip the first stitch onto the needle and purl 3 stitches on the first needle and 4 stitches on the fourth needle, turn over. Slip the first stitch onto the needle and knit the 3 stitches on the fourth needle. Work in this manner, back and forth, knitting 1 stitch more on the new round before turning. When you have knit the seventh stitch, work the remaining rows with decreases: on the next rows 6 stitches should be knit and the seventh and eighth stitches should be knit together. Turn the knitting over as usual and work the purl row as you did the knit row. Half the original number of stitches will remain on the first and fourth needles when the rounding of the heel is finished.

The heel gusset

Pick up 1 stitch through each of the 11 loops of the sides of the heel flap when the heel is finished. Pick up through the back of the loop. To avoid gaps between the first and second needles, pick up 1 or 2 more stitches. Then knit all four needles in rounds (the 11 new stitches on the fourth needle should be worked through the back of the loop to tighten the stitches). The two other needles each have 13 stitches. The 5 extra stitches on the first and fourth needles should be decreased to maintain the same number of stitches on all needles. These five stitches are called *gusset* stitches and they should be decreased by knitting the last two stitches on the first needle together and the first two stitches on the fourth needle together, separated by two plain rounds.

The length of the foot

From the beginning of the gusset to the decreasing at the toe, 54 rounds should be knit, or as many rounds as the number of cast-on stitches on three needles. An ordinary toe decreasing requires a number of rounds that relate to the number of stitches on one needle, which in this case is 18 rounds.

It is fun to think that even as far back as the fifteenth century, the foot of a stocking has been measured by wrapping it around a clenched fist. If the toe and the heel meet, the stocking will fit the foot!

Decreasing for the toe

On every other round, the last two stitches on each needle should be knit together. When 8 stitches are left, break the yarn, draw it through the stitches, and fasten the yarn end.

Rustic stockings with hourglass heels

A heel made with turned, shortened rows and without a special heel flap, is both easy and appropriate when you want to knit rustic stockings or baby socks. Because you will have a small number of stitches, a distinctly shaped heel is not required.

The distribution of the stitches should be made as usual, but with 14 stitches gathered on one needle for the heel. Knit the first row until only one stitch remains. Turn the work over and slip the first stitch onto the needle, purl the next stitches until only one stitch remains, turn over the work as before. Every time you turn the work one stitch less should be knit, until about one third of the original stitches remain – in this case four stitches.

Hourglass heel.

119

Then work one round with all four needles. At the same time, the gaps between the first and second needles and the third and fourth needles should be closed by picking up the strand of yarn between the two needles and knitting the two additional stitches turned. Knit the heel stitches only and increase stitches as you decreased earlier, as follows.

When the four middle stitches have been knit, turn the work over and slip the first stitch onto the needle; purl the remaining stitches. Knit back and forth as before; however, one more stitch should be worked before each new turn until all stitches have been knit.

Before the last turn, the two last stitches on both sides should be

late to the thickness of the foot. If the thickness is four stitches, knit as follows.

1st needle: knit until there are 4 stitches left, 2 stitches together, k2.

2nd needle: k2, 2 stitches together through back of loop, knit the remaining stitches.

3rd needle is worked as 1st needle, and the 4th needle as the 2nd needle.

Depending how flat you want the toe, you can knit more or fewer rounds between the decreases. An example of how the decreases are distributed is shown on the diagram, where the four middle stitches are not decreased, and therefore should be sewn or knit together at the very top.

Foot-shaped sock

The decreases for the toe are made to follow the shape of the foot. Decreases on the right sock are made on every round on the right side, and there are no decreases on the left side where the big toe is, until just before the closing. Reversed decreases for left sock.

Sandal socks

A big toe can be knit by working it separately with picked-up stitches between it and the other toes, as according to the method for gloves (page 110).

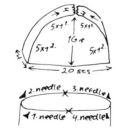

knit together to restore the original number of stitches.

Shaping the toe

To avoid having a stocking that pinches the toes, the decreases should not be made too pointed. A foot-shaped decreasing can be made so that the right and left feet are different – or if you wear sandals, you can knit a separate big toe.

The decreases for the toes should be made at the sides, so that the stitches between them re-

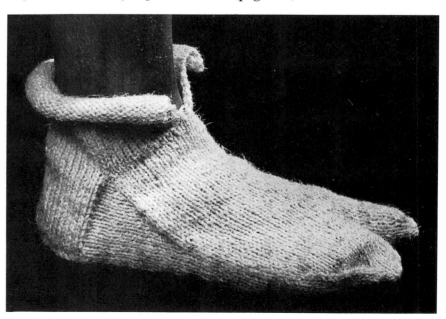

120

Leg warmers

Long, footless stockings have been used since way back in time. An executioner wearing footless hose is portrayed on an altarpiece, dated about 1435, in Boeslunde Church on Zealand. As late as World War II, fishermen from the west coast of Jutland still wore these hose.

Leg warmers are simply knit as tubes, with thin stocking yarn and decreasing at the calves. You can make a vertical slit for the heel, as in the picture of the executioner, so that only the heels and toes are bare.

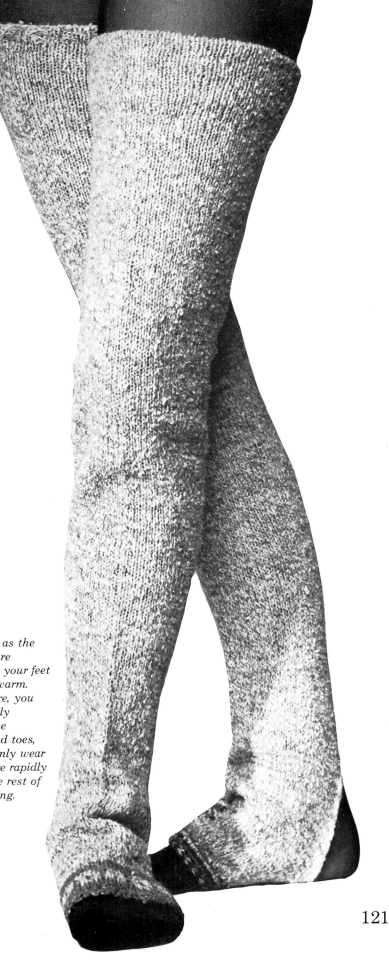

As long as the ankles are covered, your feet will be warm. Therefore, you can easily eliminate heels and toes, which only wear out more rapidly than the rest of a stocking.

121

Decorative or functional?

Small details can be of practical importance and still be decorative. Casting on with three strands of yarn, shown on page 31, will make a robust edge at the top and also enhance the beauty of the stocking. After casting on in this manner, a purled round can be worked like the purled round that completes a ribbed border. If the knit stitches are worked through the back of the loop of a stocking edge or a mitten border, the ribbing will be emphasized and will be more elastic.

The change from one row to the next can be knit as shown here to break the monotony of the knitting. The black squares represent purl stitches. Knitting in this manner has several advantages – for one thing, you can see where each

round begins and ends, which is especially important for decreasing at the back of a stocking and for the beginning of the heel; for another, you can avoid possible irregularities at the point of the change of needles.

Transverse stripes in all variations – an obvious pattern, which makes it possible to count as you knit: now there are only seven stripes to go! The foot requires eight stripes! And so on.

This decoration is often seen on the outer sides of old stockings, but the pattern has no obvious function. The side markings start as a star and continue as stripes following the outer side of the foot. Perhaps they were made to hide the changes between the third and fourth needles.

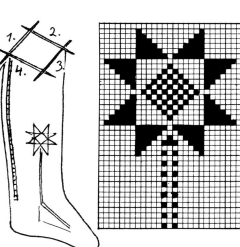

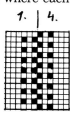

The different parts of these old Norwegian men's stockings have their own black and white patterns – the calf, the heel, the heel gusset, and so on. The decorative effect is more daring than many of the contrived modern patterns.

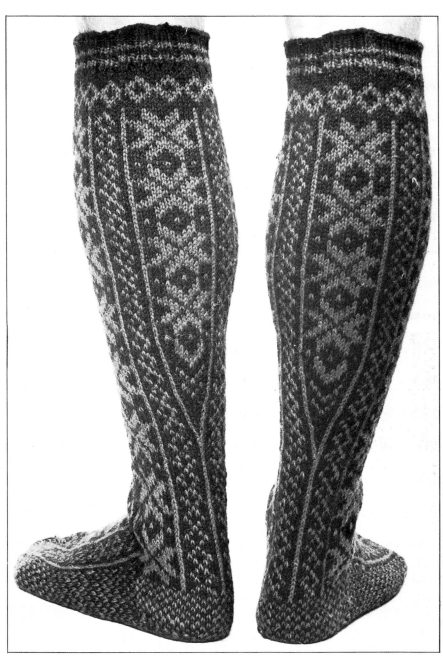

How elegant are the decreases for the calf on this pair of men's stockings from Husfliden in Norway.

Care of woollen clothes

When you have put a great deal of work into a piece of knitting, it is important to keep and treat it well. The quality will be enhanced if only you wash the garment properly.

A garment knit with thin, light, soft yarn will shrink if you wash it incorrectly. The woollen fibers will inevitably shrink and mat if the water temperature is too high, if you use too much soap, or if you wring the knitting too hard.

The simplest and most efficient way to wash wool is as follows.

Wash in several changes of water, using soap – not detergent. Carefully squeeze out the soap after each change of water. Do not rinse the wool between changes of water or after washing. Roll the garment in a towel, pressing the roll lightly, or spin dry in a washing machine. Lay the garment flat on a fresh towel to dry. *Never* tumble dry. To avoid having to press the garment with an iron, you can pat it every now and then with a flat hand. To retain the natural porosity of the wool, you can shake the work lightly when it is nearly dry.

RULES FOR WASHING

Never rub or wring.

Never shock the wool by changing from warm to cold water or vice versa.

Never put the wool in water warmer than 35°C when soap is used.

Fulling

Fulling – or matting, as it was called in early days – is a way of treating both knit and woven woollen garments to achieve fullness and softness. If you full them particularly well, the durability is increased and the clothes will be completely wind-tight and waterproof.

Fulling is a process known in all the Nordic countries. Fulled woollen clothes were worn even during the Bronze Age (around 1000 B.C.). Fulling and washing have one thing in common: soap is used for both. The difference is that when you wash a garment normally, care is taken to avoid shrinking or matting the wool by rubbing or using water that is too hot. When you full, this is exactly the result you want – that the woollen fibers more or less entangle.

The garment to be fulled should be knit looser than normal, because it will shrink noticeably.

First the garment is put into very hot water with plenty of soap,

Large numbers of woollen garments were often treated at one time by trampling them in a big vat. This treatment is still used by modern handcraft artists for woven blankets and scarves.

124

and scrubbed against a hard, grooved board. The work is now scrubbed, rubbed and kneaded until the whole piece looks sufficiently matted. Every now and then the garment should be rinsed in cold water before you continue rubbing and scrubbing. The treatment can easily take from an hour to an hour and a half. Finally, the soap is rinsed out in several changes of cold water. To soften the water, a drop of vinegar is added to the last change of rinse water.

When the clothes have dried, you can brush up the surface using a stiff brush, making it almost impossible to see that the garment has been knit.

You may be astonished to find that what normally is a deadly sin – using very hot water with a lot of soap – in this case is a virtue!

A different, and perhaps easier way, to full is with an automatic washer, not using the wool setting, but with a water temperature of about 40°C and with pure soap rather than detergent.

There is a risk, though, that the work will mat too much, because you cannot control the process. It is advisable to be careful, especially with the amount of soap, when putting your best and largest knit work in the machine to be fulled.

You should always make knitting samples first, measure the number of stitches and rows as usual, and wash some of them with other clothes. Compare the washed samples with the unwashed ones and calculate the shrinkage. The knitting can shrink as much as 5 cm across and 10 cm down. The

looser you knit, the more the work will shrink.

Concerning too much heat and wringing, you should remember that wool can be shaped by pressing it. Simply think of felt hats and tailor-made garments.

When you treat the wool, it is important that you are familiar with the quality of the wool and can make the most of its characteristics for the correct care.

RULES FOR FULLING.

The more you full, the more the wool will mat.

The more the wool is shocked from cold to hot water, the closer the fibers will lie.

The hotter the water and the more soap, the faster the wool is matted.

Index

To the left is a detail showing the decreases in the sweater's sleeve and the vertical dividing pattern.

Register of photographs

All black and white photographs, except those listed below, were taken by Jens Bull. The color photographs are by Peter Lind.

Pages 8-9 Sheep shearers on Sandø Island, the Faroe Islands. Photographed by F. Børgesen about 1900. Photo from the Nationalmuseet, Copenhagen, Denmark.

Sheep. Photo from the Historisk-Arkæologisk Forsøgscenter, Lejre, Zealand, Denmark. Photographed by Henrik Bjørslev.

Page 10 Gotlandic outdoor sheep, photographed by Peter Lind.

Page 11 Combing, photohgraphed by Henrik Bjørslev, Lejre, Zealand, Denmark.

Carding photograph from the Nationalmuseet, Copenhagen, Denmark.

Page 14 Photograph of women knitting from the Herning Museum, Jutland, Denmark.

Page 15 Two knitters from Halland, Sweden. Photographed by Victor Kinnel, Halmstad, Sweden. Photo from the Nordiska Museet, Stockholm, Sweden.

Page 21 Glove from the Kalundborg Museum, Zealand, Denmark. Photo by Peter Lind.

Page 24 Mittens from Finnmark, Norway. From the Norsk Folkemuseum in Bygdøy, Oslo, Norway. Photo by Vibeke Lind.

Page 27 Faroese fisherman photographed by Gerard Francesci.

Page 37 Madonna from a 13th-century altarpiece from Buxtehude. The altarpiece was painted by Meister Bertram and is in the Hamburger Kunsthalle, Hamburg, Germany.

Page 41 Salling dress photographed by Inga Aistrup. The dress is in the Nationalmuseet, Copenhagen, Denmark.

Red silk blouse, photographed by Ann-Mari Olsen for the Historisk Museum, Bergen, Norway.

Page 46 Flax is dried and broken. Photographed by S. Bay, Stenstrup. From the Nationalmuseet, Copenhagen, Denmark.

Page 47 Fana sweater photograph from Vestlandske Husflidslag, Bergen, Norway.

Sejrø Island sweater, knit by Niels Hansen's wife, Sejrby, toward the end of the last century. From the Kalundborg Museum, Zealand, Denmark. Photo by Peter Lind.

Sweater from Hishult, in Halland, Sweden. From the Universitetsbiblioteket in Lund, Sweden.

Page 48 Photo by Peter Lind.

Page 49 Photo of the Faroese schoolboys by press photographer Erik Petersen.

Page 50 Photo of Knud Rasmussen from the Nationalmuseet, Copenhagen, Denmark.

Page 53 Faroese sheep. Photo by press photographer Wedigo Ferchland.

Page 56 Photograph from Setesdalen, Norway. The kgl. Bibliotek, Copenhagen, Denmark.

Page 57 Peasant's louse coat from the Norsk Folkemuseum, Bygdøy, Oslo, Norway.

Page 58 Sweater knit by Professor Berit Hansen, Markaryd, Sweden. Photo by Vibeke Lind.

Page 63 The Danish Royal Family, by press photographer Allan Moe (Nordisk Pressefoto).

Page 67 Knitting border (privately owned) 2 meters long and 10 centimeters wide. The year 1815 is knit into the border.

Page 75 Milkmaid from Kvivig, Faroe Islands. Photo by F. Børgesen taken about 1900. From the Nationalmuseet, Copenhagen, Denmark.

Page 79 Tied shawl from the Stenstrup Museum, Zealand, Denmark. Photo by Peter Lind.

Page 85 Nightcap from the Varberg Museum, Sweden.

Page 102 Carving by Skjårk-Ola, 1761, from Guldbrandsdalen, Norway. From the Norsk Folkemuseum, Bygdøy, Oslo, Norway. Photo by István Rácz, Helsinki, Finland.

Embroidered gloves from Sigdal. From the Norsk Folkemuseum, Bygdøy, Oslo, Norway. Photo by István Rácz.

Page 104 The hall in Nyborg Castle, photographed by Inga Aistrup.

Mittens from Estonia. Photograph from Lietuviu Liaudies Menas, Vilnius, Lithuania.

Page 105 Mitten from Lolland, Denmark. From the Stiftsmuseet in Maribo, Denmark. Photo by Vibeke Lind.

Page 106 Mittens from Nordland, Norway, owned by Professor Berit Hansen of Markaryd, Sweden. Photo by Vibeke Lind.

Page 109 Mitten in twisted knitting, from the Norsk Folkemuseum, Bygdøy, Oslo, Norway.

Page 111 Checkered mitten from the Nationalmuseet, Copenhagen, Denmark.

Page 114 Woman, photographed by Herman Jacobsen, Copenhagen, Denmark.

Page 118 Photograph of woman from the Nationalmuseet, Copenhagen, Denmark.

Page 123 Stocking from Telemark, Norway. From the Norsk Folkemuseum, Bygdøy, Oslo, Norway.

Page 124 Milkmaid from the Faroe Islands. Photo from the Nationalmuseet, Copenhagen, Denmark.

Fulling vat from the Vordingborg Museum, Zealand, Denmark. Photo by Vibeke Lind.